Lessons from a Difficult Person, How to Deal with People Like Us
By Sarah (Sam) Elliston

Strategies to Create Change Without Trauma and Drama

The funny thing is that Sarah Elliston never realized she was a "difficult" person. A kind, but firm, boss woke her up by pointing out that she was disrupting the office camaraderie and production, as well as impeding her own professional advancement.

That began Sarah's journey to leave behind the "difficult" person and become the woman who teaches others how to deal with "difficult" people.

Sarah (Sam) Elliston now brings forth her vital manual, **Lessons from a Difficult Person: How to Deal with People Like Us**. This book ends the trauma and the drama, and minimizes the necessity of confrontation.

Elliston lays out a proven script with self-guided exercises and tools for peacefully inviting a change in the "difficult" person's behavior and demonstrates how to:

- Identify the ways to talk to a "difficult" person
- Incorporate true incentives to help people change
- Make real the consequences of the "difficult" person's action
- Increase success through acceptance and belonging

- Avoid being triggered by the "difficult" person allowing you to neutralize those hot buttons and communicate without judgment

Sam gives YOU the opportunity to take a strong, positive, confident—yet compassionate—stance with your "difficult" person.

For more information, visit www.sarahelliston.com

Praise for Lessons from a Difficult Person

Sarah Elliston draws on a lifetime of experience and courageously uses her own story to present ideas well timed for use in our current society. Her eminent descriptions of personal events and anecdotes offer skills and techniques readily adaptable and usable. The lessons learned can be implemented immediately by the reader. Individuals can use the ideas to draw closer to the people around them and thus deal with the behavior of others in ways that are empathic but not passive, assertive but not aggressive, and most of all in ways that are engaging and positive.

Robert E. Wubbolding, EdD
Director, Center for Reality Therapy

Looking back on my 30 years at Fortune 500 companies, I feel I could have helped my project teams be more successful using the insights from Sarah's book and workshops. Everyone encounters difficult people and she provides a game plan that puts the issue into perspective and provides practical steps for resolving it.

Pam Rettig, CPC

Some authors write about an issue. Sarah Elliston lived this book. And on top of that, she has studied her significant issue. She has worked with some of the top minds in Psychology and Personal Growth. The authenticity and her integrity are on every page.

Dr. Sidney B. Simon, Professor Emeritus, Psychological Education, The University of Massachusetts, Amherst

In *Lessons From A Difficult Person* Sarah Elliston never promises you that dealing with difficult people will be enjoyable or fun. What she does is give you a concise, systematic plan for having a most important conversation with a difficult person in your life.

The lessons in this empowering book unfold as Sarah shares her courageous examination of her own life as a difficult person. We learn that difficult people are often unaware that they're difficult and unaware of the impact of their behavior on others or themselves. The lessons give insight into human basic needs and emotions and are based in an in-depth understanding of Choice Theory Psychology. The lessons also offer hope and resolution.

Beyond the lessons, Sarah guides you through practical exercises that prepare you for a successful conversation. These self-guided exercises derived from Reality Therapy help formulate the conversation that betters the relationship for you and the difficult person.

When an insider expert offers me lessons, I take them and take them seriously. I highly recommend that you do, too.

Lucy Billings Robbins, Sr. Faculty, William Glasser Institute

Thank you, sweet Sarah, for writing these wise words to create solutions. Your book helps us to remember that we are creative Principle in action. We are divine, we live and move and have our being in Love. Thank you for these steps to creating At-one-ment in living our lives!

Rev. Susan EngPoole

An excellent teacher and gifted communicator, Elliston presents the concept that difficult people don't know they are difficult. Not only was this an eye opener for me, but a heart and mind opener as well. I found the self-guided exercises, examples, and recommendations for my difficult-people-interactions to be powerful and effective - so much so that I'm buying copies for every office in our organization.

Kim Brown, Counselor, Faster EFT Practioner

LESSONS FROM A DIFFICULT PERSON

How to Deal with People Like Us

Sarah H. Elliston

Lessons from a Difficult Person: How to Deal with People Like Us

Book Cover Design by Sarah Elliston and Denise Cassino
Illustrations by aksozlem4d on Fiverr.com, and from
HikingArtist.com, Adobe Stock Clip Art

Editing by Eye Comb Editors (www.eyecombeditors.com),
Proofreader's company name (sarabrown0126@gmail.com), and
Sojourn Publishing, LLC

SarahEllistonAuthor, LLC

Sarah Elliston books are available for order through Amazon.com

Visit my website: www.SarahElliston.com
Follow me on Twitter: @mainesam
Connect with me on Facebook: Sarah Elliston

Printed in the United States of America
First Printing: December 2016
Publisher: Sojourn Publishing, LLC

ISBN-13: 978-1-62747-406-1
eISBN: 978-1-62747-550-1

DEDICATION

For Kim, without whose support and care
this book never would have been written nor published.

"If you change that one little thing—to call a thing what it is instead of a problem or awful or unfortunate—what would that do to shift your experience of Infinite Energy?"
- Martha Creek

Table of Contents

FOREWORD

I had the great privilege and pleasure of a ring-side-seat as this book developed both in Sarah's mind and in various forms along the way. As you will see, Sarah (aka Sam) poured much of her life and own experience into the creation of this book. Certainly what went into making her who she is, and what became this book's message, started long before she began to write. You, fair reader, will hear stories of her childhood and adulthood, stories of others' encounters with their difficult people, as well as become the recipient of her study and practice.

The gift to me of being an eyewitness to Sam's process is the same you are about to receive if you choose to accept it; I got to put her work to work in my own life.

This book changed my thoughts about "the difficult person in my life." This book changed my understanding of myself as a difficult person. This book made me grateful for the lessons of my life and all the people who took the interest and time to help me understand myself.

If you have difficult people in your life, and who doesn't, this book will help you. If you suspect you might be a difficult person, this book will help you.

My best advice to you in either case is three things:

1. Read this book.
2. Be willing to learn the lessons about yourself that are in these pages for you.
3. Be curious about what those lessons are and get busy thinking and living differently because of them.

If there is one lesson about difficult people I hope I learned well and will never forget it is to be in their corner without attachment to how things have to look. May you find your particular lesson in these pages and watch life get easier.

Lin Schussler Williams
Indi Sales Coach; Speaker; Trainer
Author: *9 Little Words to Change Your Results*

ACKNOWLEDGEMENTS

This book would not exist without the help of Tom Bird, Mary Stevenson and Sabrina Fritts of Sojourn Publishing, LLC. Attending the writing workshop got me started but the weekly support from Tom and the consistent communications from Mary and Sabrina kept me going.

I have to thank my friends Kim Brown, Pam Rettig, Melinda Kelly, Lin Schussler-Williams, Ann Mulcahy and Villa Weisberg for their encouragement, interest, and celebrations. I have found writing can be a lonely, tiring business and they have kept me feeling human.

Thank you, Sid Simon, for nagging me for years to start writing and helping me believe I could actually do it.

Thank you, Bob Wubbolding, for continued support and important feedback over the years and especially for this book.

Thanks to Donnie Green for his consistent encouragement and boosts in keeping fit and eating healthy.

Thank you, David Thalberg, for penetrating questions and valuable branding information.

Finally, my thanks to Tori and everyone at Eye Comb Editors, who held my hand, taught me about using dashes, and edited what I wrote into a coherent, cogent piece of work.

PREFACE

Is Someone Difficult in Your Life?

Does someone drive you crazy? Is there a member of your volunteer team at church who doesn't listen? Or a coworker with a sarcastic attitude? Is it a family member who gets annoyed when they don't get their way? Is it your spouse whining? Is it someone for whom you are responsible, like a child you are raising? How about a friend of many years who is displaying some new behaviors that are causing issues between you? Or someone you supervise at work?

If so, this book is for you. It will help you identify what is going on between the difficult person and yourself. It will help you decide what to say, how to say it, and when to say it. You will have the opportunity to complete exercises, and you will, by the end of this book, have real answers.

All of us get tired of people's quirks the longer we are around them, even when we love them dearly. Sometimes we can joke about it, explain why it drives us crazy, and ask for cooperation. Sometimes we can tell ourselves to take a deep breath and practice acceptance of the things we cannot change.

However, some things we can't joke about. Sometimes the other person is an older respected member of the family or organization. It can be tough to address a behavior that you feel is hurting not just you, but the organization or customers or others in the family.

Why?

Most of us grew up with plenty of negative criticism. In their efforts to protect us and teach us to be safe and accepted in our culture, our parents and family members corrected us more times than they praised us. Even if they did compliment us on an activity, what we usually remember is the part we didn't do well.

Test it out. Remember the last time you did something of which you were proud: gave a presentation, created a new recipe for your family, made a craft as a gift for someone, or did a chore for someone like shoveling the snow or emptying the dishwasher. Got it?

Now remember the comments you received about your activity. Do you remember the praise? Can you list what you did well? Or are you like most of us—remembering the one mistake you made in your presentation or the comment from family members about dinner needing more salt? Do you remember the compliments on your quilt, or do you see the one flaw in the design? Do you remember the pat on the back, or the snow you missed that was tracked into the house? Do you remember the thanks for cleaning up, or do you remember putting the dishes away incorrectly?

A dear friend and mentor of mine, Dr. Sidney B. Simon, calls this negative selective memory the "Red Pencil

Mentality." Most of our teachers used red pencils to make corrections on our papers in school, and we have learned to go through life looking at others and ourselves through these red-pencil glasses. We believe that our job is to correct others around us, and we criticize ourselves mercilessly. In fact, most of us would never talk to another person as critically as we talk to ourselves. Because of our own self-criticism, most of us are uncomfortable thinking about giving another person criticism.

All of us have difficult people in our lives, people who are unapproachable and argumentative, need to be right all the time, complain, need to be first in situations, and create drama out of disagreements. We are taught to be polite and not hurt someone's feelings, but we are not taught how to share our frustrations with a difficult person in a way that they can actually hear.

We dance around difficulties. We don't want to confront others, and we don't want to be a bully so we label someone "difficult" and find reasons to avoid them or fire them, leaving them to continue making the same interpersonal mistakes. By not having a conversation with them, we hurt them as much as we hurt ourselves, families, colleagues, and customers.

If this avoidance describes you in any way, I congratulate you for picking up this book. You are looking for a way NOT to dance around things, NOT to hurt someone's feelings, NOT to fire someone, NOT to be a bully. You are looking for a way to openly dialogue with your difficult person.

This book contains information and strategies that you can apply to yourself and others that CAN lead to successful resolution, and create change without trauma and drama.

HikingArtist.com

Guess What? Difficult People Are Clueless

Here is the first major surprise of this book: Difficult people don't know what they are doing that annoys others because nobody has told them in a way they could hear and understand.

An interesting point about our actions is that we are least aware of what we actually do. We usually know what we are thinking and feeling while not being aware of what we are doing or saying. Yet the "doing" is the easiest part to change. It is easier to teach ourselves to floss our teeth in a new way than to teach ourselves to have a different thought or let go of a feeling.

When a difficult person doesn't know what they are doing to annoy others, they will continue to do it.

How do I know? I am a recovering difficult person.

This book describes my journey of discovering I was difficult. That experience caused me to explore what we need to ask ourselves before we talk to a difficult person so that our approach enables them to hear us, and want to change their behavior.

There Is Help Here

In this book, I share exercises for you to examine how to have a conversation with a difficult person. I describe baby steps and methods to practice, as well as examples of conversations that have taken place. At the end, I will share some successes people have had implementing these strategies in my workshops. I hope you will find an approach here that helps you feel confident working with the difficult person to find alternatives to the difficult behavior.

I am aware that you probably fear the reaction of your difficult person and, thus far, have avoided talking to them about the issue, because people avoided talking to me. The difficult person may get angry; in fact, they probably *will* get angry. I probably would have. Taking a risk in a relationship is scary. Until now, you have steered away from taking that risk.

Aren't relationships worth the risk, though? In her book, *Daring Greatly*, Dr. Brené Brown says, "But there's no equation where taking risks, braving uncertainty and opening ourselves up to emotional exposure equals weakness." (p. 32) After all, as she points out, living with courage, purpose and connection requires risk.

I'll give you tools to dare to move through the risk and develop more successful relationships. I share wisdom, ideas, and self-guided exercises that you can use to help you stay centered and sane in the face of a difficult reaction.

Remember that you are working toward a conversation, not a confrontation. Our world appears to have lost the art of dialogue. Much communication is done in sound bites, tiny tweets, and bold statements in social media. The concept of truly dialoguing is less visible in the public eye.

I anticipate that you will stand up for yourself, for the people around you, and even more, for the difficult person.

Will it work? It did with me.

I may still be considered a difficult person, but now I am open to being corrected, thinking before I speak, and sometimes, not speaking at all. I have become open to risking new friendships and meaningful relationships, most of which I lacked in the past. I feel less isolated, more accepted, and more open to being wrong.

I can't promise you that all difficult people feel the way I did, but it is my hunch that they do. I guarantee that if you dare to talk with your difficult person and stay with it, your relationship will improve.

CHAPTER ONE

HOW DID I BECOME DIFFICULT?

My name is Sarah Elliston, and I am a difficult person.

I learned that I was considered a difficult person when I was fifty years old and began to wonder why I hadn't learned it sooner. Did people never tell me, or did I not hear it? And how did I become this way in the first place? I decided to examine myself.

The Need for Belonging

I have spent most of my life believing that there was something wrong with me, and that my family didn't like me. I hoped somebody would fix me. I was born during World War II when my father was in the Navy, and my older sister Regina was two years old. She was a happy, outgoing, cheerful child and she and my mother had a pretty good time before I was born. I came along, and I was noisy and wanting to be the center of attention. Suddenly Regina had competition. She became a quiet, spiteful child, correcting me continuously and, in my perception, finding fault with everything I did.

Two pictures in my infancy predominate: the first is the fact that my mother was breastfeeding. The accepted medical approach at the time was to nurse only every four hours, in order to instill early discipline in the child. My mother, being the college educated child of two educators, strived to do the informed thing—what the doctors currently advised. She told me later that Dr. Spock told mothers to have their babies cry for an hour before nursing, and described to me how we agonized for that hour. I can only imagine the tension that she and Regina lived with as I cried. Then she would isolate herself with me, since in those days, breastfeeding wasn't done with others present. Now, I sympathize with both of them. It must have been awful. As for me, the hungry child, I took on a core belief that the only way to get what you need is to cry and cry.

The second significant picture is of my mother reading and playing with Regina as I peered through a door from a playpen in another room. I was supposed to have my quiet time so she could have her time with Regina. As she told me, after my son was born, "You hated being in that playpen. You howled and cried and threw things. It was a disaster." (Ironically, she was suggesting at the time that I use a playpen for my child.) The playpen taught me that there must be a reason I was excluded; there must be something wrong with me. I wasn't allowed to be with the rest of the world unless I raised the roof. Thus I learned the only way to feel included and acknowledged was to make a lot of noise.

Regina not only played the big-sister role of telling me what to do, but she was also skillful in saying things that made me feel wrong most of the time. She was the master of sarcastic comments and negative criticism. My memory of our childhood was a struggle to get the best of her, as she appeared to do effortlessly to me. She was my authority and managed to damage many of my beliefs that I had a right to be happy in the world.

I was born on Halloween. When I was seven, the neighborhood families gathered at our house for a potluck supper as the sun was going down so all the trick-or-treaters could go together. I was very excited because it was my birthday and we were having a party. I was going to have a birthday cake and presents. Regina looked at me from her superior age of nine and said, "They aren't coming for you. You are not important. They are coming to eat and go trick-or-treating. You're so stupid. You think everything is about you."

As an adult, one could laugh at the comment and speculate that the speaker must be unhappy, but as a child, it engraved in me the belief there was nothing special about me. They had other reasons for coming to "my" party. I knew by then that my sister didn't like me and that other children seemed to like her. If they liked her then they must not like me; there was something wrong with me.

Regina and I argued and fought, in some form of competition all our lives. Our younger sister, Karen, went along with whatever was going on and played with Regina so that it always felt to me that it was two against one. Sometimes when my parents went out for the evening and we had a babysitter, they would sneak into my room in the dark to scare me. They would growl, "Garr, garr!" and I would be terrified. The sitter wouldn't know, and I would feel helpless. The few times I tried to turn the tide and sneak into Regina's room, she and Karen were waiting for me and jumped out and yelled, "Garr, garr!" first.

Consequently, my life experience with women was that when we were in trios, I automatically felt separate.

I had cousins, with whom I would sometimes stay when my family would go skiing over a weekend. There were five children in their family, and they all seemed to like each other. Their house was near our church, and I much preferred to stay home to sing in the choir rather than travel in the car for hours with my sisters, feeling unwanted.

When I stayed over, my uncle made quite a fuss over me and my opinions, even though he had daughters of his own. I felt very much loved in their house. I longed to be part of my cousins' family and loved being with them. Once, when I was in high school, my parents traveled out of town for two weeks, and I was able to live at my cousins' house and go to school from there. It was heaven.

Dr. William Glasser would say that my cousins' family met my need for belonging and connecting. It was a picture of how I wished to live all the time. Dr. Glasser, creator of Choice Theory and Reality Therapy, tells us that we are born with genetic instructions of needs to be met and we act on the outside world to achieve them. The most important need is to feel a sense of belonging. I yearned to feel it at my home, and felt that way at my cousins' home.

Dr. Glasser states that all behavior is purposeful, designed to meet the need for belonging and four other needs: the need to have a sense of making choices (freedom), a need for fun and joy, a need for physical survival and health, and a need for a sense of achievement and empowerment. Everything we do is an attempt to meet one or more of these five basic needs. Being with my cousins was fun as well as a place where I felt a sense of belonging.

When I wasn't at somebody else's house, I found my sense of connection in books and other hobbies. I have always been a voracious reader. I could escape into the books where people had companions and allies who helped them face challenges. I especially liked the series of biographies on famous people. These stories described the individuals as children, and how they grew and became remarkable as adults. They felt like my friends.

Besides books, I was lucky that I went to summer camp from the age of eight to sixteen and found friends and fun there while I was developing other skills. I rode horses, swam, played tennis, danced ballet, sang in the chorus, hiked, canoed and sailed. At twelve, I attended a camp where I learned to speak, sing, and think in French. I continued at this camp until I was a junior counselor there at age eighteen. Most importantly, people liked me at camp. I received honors at camp, I had friends at camp, and nobody criticized me there. I felt connected at summer camp.

What I now realize is that I met many of my needs away from my family. I was successful in school and had friends and activities. Yet at my core, because of the family lack of validation, I still felt something was wrong with me.

As adults, Karen and I have talked about the dynamics of our family. She concurred that she and Regina bullied me. She explained that she didn't want Regina to treat her the way she saw me being treated, so she played with Regina most of the time. She was also five years younger than Regina, and the age difference helped create safety. I didn't always want to do things the way Regina directed me and she would tell me that I couldn't play with them. I tried to fight back, but she told me that if I didn't do it her way I couldn't come into her room; I couldn't play with her and my younger sister.

I remember a time when I went to my mother, who was cooking supper—not her favorite activity. I begged her for help, asking her to talk to my sisters and make them include me in their game. I remember crying and saying, "They are always so mean to me." Her frustrated and frazzled end-of-the-day comment was, "I can't fight your battles for you. You are going to have to figure this out for yourself."

This was the cap on my belief that there was something wrong with me. I have never forgotten it, although my mother would be horrified that this is what I remember about my childhood. She certainly showed me that she loved me in other ways. But in this instance, I discerned that I wasn't worth advocating for, and I wasn't smart enough to figure it out myself. My solution was to find a book to read, and that is most often what I did whenever I didn't have someone to play with. We would sometimes have my friends over but, more often, I would go to spend the afternoon or the night at a friend's house.

When I was with my mother, alone, we talked about boys and school and my friends, and I would tell her my secrets. Later, when Regina and I were arguing about something, my mother would interject a remark referring to something I had told her in confidence. It usually supported Regina's point, and I felt betrayed.

Besides books, I found that I was more comfortable with boys than girls and I was always surprised and pleased when they liked me. I attended a girls private school and got to know boys at private schools, and we communicated through snail mail. I remember at one time I was writing to seven boys at seven different schools, and one day I arrived home to find seven letters, one from each boy. I thought this was a great achievement. They MUST like me. I was liked!

My mother commented, "Isn't that a little shallow, dear? How can you have so many superficial relationships?" I hadn't experienced them as superficial and was devastated that she didn't recognize my gifts of being friendly and having the ability to write. Then my mother acknowledged that she was a little jealous of my popularity. She hadn't had any boyfriends in school. I remember feeling compassion for her unhappy teen years, but never forgot that her first thought about me was that I was shallow. It felt like a mixed message of, "Oh, look at you doing what I couldn't do, but it isn't really a good thing to do." It told me that there was something wrong with me.

My perception as an adult is that our house had less conflict in it when I wasn't there. I didn't really fit there. One of the activities that we did together on vacation was to play cards in the evening. My father's favorite game, and thus everybody else's favorite game, was Russian Bank. This was a form of double solitaire where each player took turns to build up all the suits in the center of the table. The challenge of the game was to see where the other player made a mistake during his turn and yell, "Stop!" Then it would become your turn. I hated the idea of having somebody critically observing me while I was playing, and that the purpose of the game was to catch someone making a mistake. I had enough criticism in my life. I refused to play and would read a book instead.

I often felt at odds with my father. He was a private, thoughtful man who preferred peace and quiet. I am an extroverted thinker which means every thought was spoken until, as an adult, I (finally) learned it really annoys people. I had questions, comments, and thoughts, and I felt compelled to share them. He liked to walk in the woods, quietly. So I was welcome, if I didn't talk. He enjoyed canoeing, and I was invited, if I was silent. I enjoyed being with him, but I wanted to talk and connect with him.

He loved to sail and most often sailed and raced on a small lake. The wind was never steady so his instruction to me in the boat was to "hold your breath," so he could catch the next breeze. What he meant was, "sit still and don't talk." I wanted to spend time with my father but felt awkward and unwelcome—I couldn't talk, and I couldn't move. Also, I was often scared when the boat heeled over in order to sail quickly. He wanted to win the race, and that seemed more important than me.

His other sport was skiing, and for that, we would drive for five hours to New Hampshire. When we traveled anywhere in the car, he told me to "put a cork in it," because he wanted quiet. I was much too young to appreciate the stress of his job and the rejuvenation that occurred when we were not talking. I admired my father, but felt he preferred Karen because she was silent. As an adult, I was able to sail with him and walk in the woods with him for long stretches of quiet, and after he retired, he became much chattier, but when I was a child, it appeared he only enjoyed my company if it seemed I wasn't there.

Unfelt Affection

Amazingly, Karen and Regina feel that my mother's focus was all on me. They saw her spending her entire time trying to fix me and make me happy. I had numerous problems. I was too skinny and had to have special vitamins in chocolate milk every day. They were not allowed to drink chocolate milk every day because of the sugar. When Mom took Regina to see a child psychiatrist for being too withdrawn, the doctor reported that Regina was fine, but Sarah sounded really interesting. So, I visited the child psychiatrist every month from age eight to twelve.

I was the only one of us who had to have braces on my teeth. This involved my mother driving into the city every week and then every month for a few years. My mother knew my interests and had me enrolled in special drama classes and ballet. Neither of my sisters did any of these things, so to them, it looked as if I got all the attention.

There were moments of harmony among us and the ones I cherish occurred when we sang rounds in the car. My mother would be driving with the three of us in the station wagon, and we would sing rounds where one of us would start the song, and then another would start it and then another join in and another. I loved the tonalities of the songs, "White Sands and Grey Sands," "White Choral Bells," and "Orleans, Beaugency, Notre Dame de Paris." I can feel the joy of those moments singing together. The most dramatic memory was when we drove around the city of Boston on the new circle highway from the south shore to the north shore, during Hurricane Carol in 1954. My grandmother was by herself in a house on the north shore and my mother was worried about her. We sang rounds all the way, instinctively ducking when we saw tree limbs bending outside the car. It was a dramatic trip.

I now realize that my mother did work hard to help me be happy. One summer at camp I danced the role of the Firebird in a ballet routine to Stravinsky's *The Firebird Suite*. I came home loving the music and the dance. She gave me the recording of it and helped me move furniture around so that I could dance around our living room. I remember doing it many times, sometimes when she was cooking supper. I wasn't doing it to be watched; I just loved doing the dance.

Besides taking me to the psychiatrist, driving back and forth for braces, and making sure I went to camp every summer, my mother read aloud to me every night until I was in high school. Even though I devoured books on my own, I loved sitting with her in the evenings when she read aloud. She had a great reading voice, and I felt a connection when she read to me. I owe my ability to write to her. My secondary school required an essay every weekend, and on Sunday afternoon (on the weekends when we weren't skiing), I would read my papers to her, and she would patiently help me identify topic sentences and move paragraphs around so the essay made sense. A sweet memory of her is, later, when I wrote a paper for an Asian Studies Seminar for my master's degree. This was the pre-computer age. I mailed her the pages, and she corrected them and mailed them back. Then she typed the final draft. She said she loved learning such detail about China and Chou En-lai.

When I was in the ninth grade, my teachers suggested I might be happier in a boarding school, so my mother and I visited three of them in surrounding states. I liked them all and couldn't decide which to attend. Then, when I told my classmates and teachers that I was leaving, they all expressed sadness and appealed to me not to leave. I was torn because I hadn't realized they liked me. I eventually told my mother she had to decide. She decided that I would stay home.

I have often wondered if we might have been happier if I had spent my high-school years as a boarding student away from my family. Despite the fact that my mother accommodated so many of my wishes, and said she wanted me to be home instead of away at school, I was aware that I was a lot of trouble.

Crying an hour for nourishment and raising the roof to escape the isolation of my playpen left me with deeply ingrained habits that made me a thorn in everyone's side. I felt invisible to my father and rejected by my siblings. So despite my mother's efforts, I never fit in my family. I felt unwelcome from day one, and it has led to a lifelong inner distrust and inner pain.

Was There a Fix?

Managing to hide much of this inner self-distrust, I graduated from college and started teaching school. I met a man freshly-returned from Vietnam and we spent his leave together. We ended up falling in love, and I distinctly remember thinking that, with his love and wisdom, I would be okay. I would have someone who would listen and care for me and help me fight the demons inside. Essentially, I thought, he would fix me.

My now ex-husband is a wonderful man with great tenderness and caring, but he was a recently-returned vet and did not share his innermost thoughts easily. I eventually learned that he shared his joy and pain through art or music or walking in the woods, but I was more direct and demanding.

An important moment for me occurred during our honeymoon. We were driving across the country and as I drove I was trying to explain why I felt so outside of my family and how hurt I had been. I thought my information was like gold to my new husband; he would help me stop feeling this way. As a scientist, he had often pointed out flora and fauna—for example, different hawks that we saw, or a new variety of rock or trees as we moved through different land formations. I had listened with interest.

But as I expounded on my pain, he interrupted, pointing out the window.

"Cow," he said.

"Cow?" I thought. "What? Did he think I had never seen a cow?" I was stunned that the cow was more important than my emotional pain. He was probably trying to distract me from feeling the pain, but I remember feeling that, as nice as he was, he couldn't understand me and he wasn't going to fix me. I wondered what I was supposed to do now, since my husband couldn't make me okay.

I had developed into a person who spoke her own mind, all the time, who argued with authority and made sure I got the last word. The year our son was born, we did some additions to our house so we would have a second bedroom, a study, and a laundry room on the second floor. It was my first experience of remodeling, and it provided a perfect example of how I made myself "heard." We had designed a full bath on the back of the house and the plan called for a window in the outside wall. Once the actual construction got underway, the architect and contractor discovered that the water pipes would also be running along the wall. Their solution was to put the tub and shower along the wall—hence, no window. I said, "No, all bathrooms need a window to allow steam and other smells to go outside." The men went through the logical explanation about costs and savings, and my husband agreed we would have to sacrifice the window.

I responded with logic, and then melted down. I raised my voice and tearfully pointed out that some of the money came from me and I had as much of a voice as my husband did. I screamed that, as typical men, they were not thinking about living in the bathroom, but thinking about the easiest way to solve the problem. I raved, pointing out that the architect should have figured out the dilemma before we started. Wasn't that what he was paid for? I was rude, argumentative, and difficult. I remember feeling dismayed that I had to scream and cry for them to consider my point of view as credible. I was as enraged about having to have a tantrum to be "heard" as I was about the idiocy of building a bathroom without a window.

I got my window in the bathroom and they designed a bench to cover the pipes. It turned out to be a great place for a small wet person to dry off after a bath in winter, since hot water ran through the pipes. My husband told me that I had been right, it was the best way to have the bathroom, and he was grateful that I stuck to my guns. Sadly, I couldn't appreciate the compliment, and never forgot the feeling of rage at the three men against me who kept saying, "You don't understand. It's the savings that are important." I felt that I had to have a fit of temper to be heard. I see a connection between my defensiveness and the feeling of hostility in my childhood home. My instinct has been to distrust and then use rage as protection.

I spent considerable time talking to a variety of therapists, which led me to a variety of self-help activities. When our son was born and I didn't want to spank him, I studied Parent Effectiveness Training. I liked it so much that I became an instructor and taught a number of classes. They helped my husband and me communicate more effectively, and I found I didn't have to spank my son.

When I was fired from a job because of my tone of voice, my boss suggested I work for the jails because I could confront people there. He suggested that I learn Reality Therapy because he heard it was a direct approach and I was direct. I followed up on it even though I was pretty sure I didn't want to be a therapist. I discovered a respectful environment with fascinating information about how people learn and change. I studied Dr. Glasser's Choice Theory and Reality Therapy and became certified in that process too. I found that teaching it is fun and keeps me focused on being responsible for my behavior. I have been teaching it for over thirty years. Keeping the concepts in mind has helped me be less critical of others and the success of my students is always rewarding. PET and Reality Therapy may not have been the "fix" I was looking for, but they kept me moving in the right direction.

How Did I Survive?

I had significant support from age thirty-five to fifty by attending workshops in Values Realization, led by Dr. Sidney B. Simon, Professor Emeritus at the University of Massachusetts. These workshops taught skills of clarifying values by examining the way we wanted to live and what we were actually doing. Dr. Simon is a master facilitator. Once, I watched him skillfully transform a room full of skeptical journalists into a classroom of eager students. He creates a workshop environment for everyone that is safe, where real issues can be examined without judgment or criticism.

In his workshops, we only knew each other's first names, and we didn't talk about our careers because it allowed us to be ourselves without labels. We were discouraged from attempting to do therapy on each other but encouraged to be responsible for our own personal work. There was music and massage and trust building. I found myself feeling as if I was at summer camp in this environment. I didn't feel as if there was something wrong with me. All my needs were met in these workshops. I attended at least one week-long workshop a summer. I learned to play guitar so I could lead the singing with which we began each session, I became a trainer in Values Realization, and for two years I was president of an institute created to carry on the work. My husband and son came to the workshops, and the music and strategies became part of our lives. I started to sing again. A major result was that I was able to quit smoking. These workshops where I felt loved, accepted, and applauded, where I got to look at my life without criticism, and where I learned life strategies, kept me sane through these years.

Another result was that, at age forty-four, I realized that I was attempting to cover my feelings and pain with alcohol, and I became sober in a Twelve-Step program. It was a humbling experience where I found myself learning, every day, that I wasn't in charge of the world. I had friends around me who reminded me that I could learn how to feel—sober—one day at a time. They pointed out that I had feelings other than anger and invited me to explore them. I started to understand that my opinions were just that; not laws of government or laws of physics. I might actually be wrong about a few things. I had always believed there was something wrong with me, but I began to see that I could be flawed and still be okay.

CHAPTER TWO

WHY DID I CHANGE?

The Conversation That Started It All

At the age of fifty, I had a new boss, Denise, whom I greatly admired. She gave me glowing compliments on my training skills and other talents, and she mentioned that there was one issue she wanted to raise. She said, "Sarah, there's this thing you do when you're stressed, and it is really distracting for the rest of us. It changes the energy of our workspace, and I'd like you to stop."

I had no idea what she was talking about. Not a clue. Nor did I realize where it would lead me.

Since I wasn't aware of what I was doing, we agreed that the next time I was doing whatever it was, she would tell me.

A week or so later at work, I couldn't find my brand new glasses. They were my first pair of reading glasses, and they were expensive. I had placed them in my purse, had driven out for fast food, hadn't gotten out of the car, hadn't even opened my purse because I had money in my pocket, had driven back to the office, had come in, had opened my purse—no glasses. I was stumped. I dumped out my purse, no glasses. I checked coat pockets, no glasses. I pulled out my chair, my computer, moved everything around on my desk, picked up folders, dropped them, muttered to myself, and finally went out and checked the car. No glasses. I was seriously frustrated and I stomped back into our office area, a series of five cubicles in a smallish room, and started to go through all the things on my desk again. Full of rage and scared that I had lost these new, expensive glasses, I was saying things like, "Damn it! This is crazy; I never even opened my purse. Where the hell did they go, for God's sake?"

Denise leaned out her door and said, "Sarah, can I see you for a sec?" I stepped in, and she closed the door and said, "That. What you are doing right now. It has to stop."

I gaped at her, "What am I doing?"

She stated calmly, "You are stomping around the office area, muttering under your breath, lifting things up and dropping them, pushing your chair in and out, opening drawers and closing them violently—it's clear you are frustrated and angry—it's a mini-tantrum, and it is creating tension in the whole office. We can't do our jobs with such negative energy. It needs to stop."

I was floored. Dumbfounded. I was totally unaware of what I was doing or that any of the people around me were even noticing. I was caught up in my snit fit and completely lost in my own frustration. I remembered a tenet of the Twelve-Step program which states, "When we were wrong, we promptly admitted it." I realized that here, I was clearly wrong.

I think I said something like, "Well, I don't want to ruin the energy. I apologize. I'm sorry, everybody, if I have made it hard for you to do your work." I sat down in my office, never did find the glasses, and I looked at myself.

My heart sank, and I feared losing my job. Who has raging outbursts at age fifty? Had this been happening for a long time? Am I some kind of complete failure who alienates the world by getting angry at the drop of a hat? I feared the answer was yes.

Development Demystified

A few weeks later I visited my mother, who was in her eighties, living in a lovely retirement community to which she had moved when my father died. They had been married for fifty years, and she missed him. She seemed well-liked by the other residents, had friends in the community, and participated in volunteer and community activities. However, in private, she often complained bitterly to me and my sisters that she was still angry that he had died and left her alone.

During my visit with her, she started to talk to me about a school she had attended where she had been miserable. This had been more than sixty years before. She slammed her hand down on her chair, turned to look at me with a furious, livid look and said, "Do you know? The nerve of them? I hated that school and they asked me for money. Honestly! Those students called me names and were so mean. For God's sake, I'd like to call them and give them a piece of my mind. The unmitigated gall! It makes me so mad I could just scream." She stood up and stomped out of the room, grumbling to herself.

A light bulb came on. I watched my mother have a mini-tantrum and realized that this was the norm. I had seen her do it all my life. I hadn't noticed it as unusual before. No wonder she hadn't taught me not to do this. I learned my lesson well. I wasn't flawed, merely well-taught.

Back at my bed and breakfast, I called my son. "Do I do this? Is this something that you have seen me do?" He replied that I had been doing it all his life. He reminded me of the time I threw his riding toy down the stairs and broke it in a fit of rage and tears. "Remember? Daddy took it and put it back together, and we just went on. It is just who you are, Mom." I asked him if it troubled him or if it bothered him. He replied that he had gotten used to it, and didn't mind, but that it sometimes freaked out his friends.

I hadn't known I was exhibiting this kind of melt-down behavior on a regular basis. I wasn't aware of doing it nor was I aware of the impact it had on others. I asked my son, "Were you scared of me?" He said, "No. You just have a walloping temper and, you know, Dad and I just learned to stay out of your way. Five minutes later it was as if it had never happened." I suddenly remembered my mother being so angry at one of my playmates when he broke a special glass that she exclaimed, "God damn your soul to hell on wheels, by jet!" and how it ended my birthday party. She was surprised and disappointed that soon afterward the parents took their children home.

We were both difficult and didn't know it.

Without Denise, I might never have learned it. Why hadn't anybody else ever said anything?

23

I wondered if others had been bothered by it—obviously, they had; I had been fired from a teaching job and an administrative job for saying the wrong thing to the wrong person, and both times I had been angry. Something about my tone, they said. Now I realized I had had little temper fits on the job.

They felt as natural to me as breathing. And I didn't know I was doing it.

Do we know what we are doing? Are we aware of what we do with our faces, with our hands, how we hold our bodies? Recall that Dr. Glasser points out that we are least aware of our actions, and yet they are the easiest things to change. It is easier to do something different than to feel something different.

Most people are familiar with body language, and we learn to read it. We know that arms folded in front means defensiveness, feeling threatened, while arms open at your sides usually means comfortable, open to the situation. I began to wonder what I had missed in reading other people's body language in their reactions to me. I hadn't even been aware of my own body language.

I don't think I am so incredibly different. Many "difficult" people in the world feel detached or unconnected in some way, and wonder why others seem to have closer, more substantial friendships. They are exhibiting behaviors that are labeled "difficult" without any awareness of what they are doing and without any understanding of the impact. Apparently, no one has ever said, "Hey, would you stop that?" in a way they could both hear and find themselves interested in heeding. If people tried, it felt like negative criticism, which merely brought defensiveness.

Why hadn't anybody told me?

I started by asking myself, "How would *I* talk to a difficult person about this?" and began to explore what I knew about how to talk to difficult people in a way that might lead to change. I took information I had learned from Dr. Thomas Gordon, Dr. William Glasser, and Dr. Sidney B. Simon, and developed a workshop to explore some ideas. I invited others to attend these workshops to identify what might work with difficult people and received feedback that it was helpful. When I announce a workshop for dealing with difficult people, it fills up, revealing that almost everybody has a difficult person in their life. It seems that dealing with difficult people the way Denise dealt with me is very unusual, due to fear of a negative reaction. So I tried to think about what worked with me and have taught this to others while learning from them.

CHAPTER THREE

GIVE US A CLUE

Still looking at behavior, I discovered that other people had tried to explain the problems with my behavior to me. Long before I met Denise, my first supervising teacher was a happy, energetic woman named Dorothy. She laughed and enjoyed life, and I knew on the first day I met her that I wanted to be just like her. I worked with her for five years. I learned most of what I knew about being a teacher from her. My favorite story of her was when she was coming down the stairs in the morning, carrying Christmas presents, and she tripped, watching them fall down the stairs. Her response as she lay on the stairs was to laugh, and she laughed when relating the story. I longed to be able to respond to stress with laughter.

Considering my desire to walk in her shoes, one of the most painful and devastating days of my life occurred when she told me not to apply for her job after she retired. She hadn't ever described any negative behavior in our reviews. She'd said things like, "I have a sister like you and I understand you." I thought that was lovely; I liked being understood.

Her reviews had been positive, although sometimes she would suggest that I might learn how to communicate better. This always puzzled me since I thought I was a pretty good communicator. I thought I expressed myself well. I didn't think anybody had any doubt about what I thought and why.

That day, Dorothy told me that I shouldn't apply for her position as supervising teacher because both principals to whom she had reported in the last five years had begged her to get rid of me, find me another job somewhere else— just get me out of their school. They wanted me fired. They wanted her to do it and she wouldn't because I was so good at my job.

I had a physical reaction as if I had been hit. I felt confused, angry, disappointed, and deceived. Stunned. I remember crying for an hour. "Why?" I kept asking her. What on earth was so wrong with me and why hadn't she told me?

Dorothy explained that the principals felt my tone of voice when asking questions was argumentative and threatening. I was surprised that some of her examples were times that I thought I had been articulate and had really participated in the meetings. Even though we all learned from my questions, there was a kind of a "bite" to them. My tone and approach to working with authority was confrontational and they didn't like it.

In her reviews, she had been unable to articulate what they wanted me to change, partially because she disagreed. I was just like her older sister and she didn't find me difficult or threatening at all.

I was shocked. As she explained more and more, I felt betrayed. I had been in a bubble for five years, going along doing my job, thinking everything was all right, when these people, and probably others, had been watching me and wishing I was gone. I came away from the conversation with an altered view of Dorothy. I had so admired her, but I felt a new sense of disillusionment I hadn't felt before.

Her not telling me meant that I had spent years infuriating the leaders of my school. Her telling me left me shell-shocked and wondering if I should quit. I wondered if I could get along with anybody. I wondered how to forgive her. I wondered if I could change and began to try, moment by moment, to talk to others without sounding argumentative. I acknowledged that I was more direct than many others, but I tried to become agreeable and quiet, as much as possible.

Until Dorothy was forced to share the impact of my behavior and the consequence, she hadn't felt comfortable talking about it.

This conversation occurred in March, and when Dorothy retired in June, she complimented me on how much I had changed and what positive feedback she had received about me. She was really pleased. At the time I wanted to say, spitefully, "If you had told me five years ago, I would have changed five years ago." It is clear, however, that I hadn't completely changed because my unspoken comment was so filled with resentment. The saving grace, to me, was that I didn't actually say it.

As I have continued searching for why I didn't understand what people were trying to tell me, I recalled that I was once told during a review for another job that I acted inappropriately at staff meetings. I asked for specifics and learned later that requesting clarification was actually considered "difficult" because I didn't just agree and say, "Okay."

My supervisor mentioned a question I had asked at a staff meeting six months before. I frowned, trying to remember the incident, the question. My immediate response was "Why are you only telling me now? Why didn't you tell me then?" That was also considered "difficult." My supervisor explained that the boss had felt challenged and sent a memo that my questions were inappropriate and she should take action.

I stared at her. "Do you remember this?" I asked. Yes, she did. She pointed out that I had sounded angry at the announcement of a change in a program and had argued for its continuing. "I do remember feeling passionate about it. So what did I do that was inappropriate?" I asked. Her response was that that kind of passion was not suitable in the staff meetings and I should come to her when I felt strongly about things. She enjoyed my passion, but it disrupted the meetings.

So, in this case, passion became identified as "difficult" even though I didn't realize it at the time. I probably sounded angry when I asked why a program was being discontinued, and she called it passion. I thought passion was a good thing so I was confused by the whole conversation. I didn't hear something that I could really understand.

When Denise, years later, confronted me about tantrums, I understood, but I wondered why no one had ever told me about that behavior. Looking back, I can see that it was part of what my supervisor had meant by passion. It's been suggested that anger and passion are two sides of the same coin; positive and negative polarities. I wish I had heard this earlier in my life.

At the time, I thought if passion was inappropriate, why hadn't I heard about it? I first asked my husband if he had noticed it, and he replied he had learned to let me roar around because it would be over quickly and I would forget it happened. He reminded me of the incident with the bathroom window.

I was devastated.

A portion of the hurt was suspecting that I had been pushing people away for years with this behavior. I am probably not alone in this characteristic of being a difficult person. It's important to be approachable in one's job, and I felt I had worked hard at being friendly. However, because of my emotional outbursts, people almost certainly avoided me.

Another example of what happens when people avoid the conversation happened to a professional colleague of mine. A senior administrator in his organization refused to allow the women in his department to wear pants to work. He had grown up in a different country and felt it was inappropriate when women wore long pants instead of skirts. This was 1998, so all the women in the other departments were wearing pants to work.

My colleague didn't know if anybody had a conversation with the administrator or what discussion might have occurred. What he did know was that his agency ended up creating a committee with representative staff from every department, which met for two years, once a month, for an hour or two. The result was a dress code for the company that permitted women to wear pants.

My colleague was dismayed that his agency had so many employees spend time developing this dress code simply because no one communicated clearly with the administrator. The loss in productivity and impact on morale was incalculable.

I saw it as the result of someone being unwilling to have the conversation long enough, with enough compassion and conviction, to help the administrator identify some needed changes. I am sure many organizations do the same thing: spend hours of time creating a systemic change that one person could influence with a conversation with a difficult person.

CHAPTER FOUR

WHAT'S REALLY GOING ON?

Objectively Describing Behavior

I always start by asking "What bothers us about difficult people? What are the difficult people doing?" Recall how you describe your difficult person. Typical responses are: controlling, manipulative, rude, bossy, narcissistic, angry, picky, and passive-aggressive. Unfortunately, these descriptions are actually judgments about other people's behavior, not really descriptions of behavior. The negative terms we use to describe what we don't like represent our emotional reaction to their behavior—not really their behavior.

Denise didn't say, "Sarah, you are acting like a bratty, selfish child, completely ignoring other people's needs." That would have been a judgment about what I was doing. She said, "You are stomping around the office area, muttering under your breath, lifting things up and dropping them."

I like to look at behavior as something you can hear a person say or see a person do. A clinical psychologist named Dr. Thomas Gordon shared this definition for parents of teens who had sent their kids to him for help. As they got better, they would stop seeing Dr. Gordon. Six months later the parents would call and ask him to fix their kid again. He realized that the parents needed the help. His Parent Effectiveness Training became very popular and successful. The book is still published and used.

I found that the ability to identify my son's specific behavior of slamming the door, leaving the dirty plate on the table, and leaving dirty socks on the floor, helped me communicate what I wanted to be different without subjecting him to negative criticism.

Describing the behavior of a difficult person requires letting go of our negative judgments of them and becoming very concrete about what is said and what is done. We aim at a position of neutrality in describing the behavior so that we can remain unemotional in our conversation. In the workshops that I lead on this topic, we spend a good deal of time on this activity because it isn't anything most of us have been taught. Our culture labels and judges everything.

We describe behavior with the negative reaction we have for the behavior, not the actual behavior itself. We have been taught to label behavior as good or bad or controlling or empowering, and that can poison our capacity to describe the behavior without a judgment.

Another element of the judgment we may be making has to do with bias. We have cultural biases of which we may not be aware. They can influence our perception of a behavior or of an impact. I saw this in my own life when I had a roommate who was African American, and she invited me to celebrate a holiday with her family. We were all women in the room, and the conversation got louder and louder, and I noticed that I was uncomfortable. My cultural experience was that voices are only raised in anger. Theirs wasn't. They expressed joy and pleasure in each other much more loudly than I was used to. I told myself that they weren't arguing—this wasn't a hostile environment— it was a party. This was how they celebrated. As I began to understand, I became more comfortable.

I could have become condemning and critical. Because I knew they were acting to meet their needs, the same needs as mine, I was able to eliminate any judgment. In order to prepare for a conversation with our difficult person, we need to look to our description of behavior and its impact to make sure it is free of judgment and bias. If we feel judgment about their behavior the difficult person will know it and everything we say will be received as negative criticism.

What about Motivation?

Dr. William Glasser has determined that everything we do is purposeful. We do what we think will fulfill our needs. This behavior includes doing, thinking, feeling and physiology. As I mentioned before, Dr. Glasser developed Choice Theory which teaches that we are born with genetic instructions to fulfill five needs: the need to belong and feel a part of something; the need to have fun and joy in life; the need to have a sense of choice and freedom in one's life; the need to achieve, stand out, and be empowered; and the need to procreate, be healthy, and survive.

These needs are in our brains from birth, and everything we do is designed to fulfill one or more of them. The needs are the same for all of us, but what we think will meet the needs is different for all of us. We do what we have seen or learned will bring us something close to what will meet our needs. The fact that we often do things that have the opposite effect doesn't always mean we change, especially if it is all we know how to do. It gets a result that *feels* fulfilling, and we keep doing it.

As part of your preparation for a conversation, practice thinking a little differently about the people we identify as difficult:

- We may label someone as difficult because they talk all the time because they are trying to connect. Their behavior is purposeful. They are attempting to meet their need to feel a part of the group, yet we wish they would stop monopolizing the discussion.
- We might describe someone with strong opinions as boorish and controlling. Again, this individual may be attempting to meet a need for belonging by sharing their ideas. They may also be trying to meet the need for empowerment by hoping they are adding important information to the conversation or discussion.
- We might describe someone as a rebel, a person who refuses to follow directions, and they may be attempting to meet a need for freedom. Yet our preference is to avoid them because they don't do what they are told.
- A colleague who argues emphatically for a particular program may be labeled as disruptive and not a team player. They may be attempting to meet a need for freedom or for a sense of achievement. If they are responsible for the threatened program, they may be attempting to meet a need for survival, to keep their job.
- We might call someone a slacker who isn't serious and makes everything a joke, and they may be attempting to meet their need for fun and joy in

their life. We might start to feel uncomfortable, believing that they don't take life as seriously as we do.

- A person we might label as egotistical may be attempting to meet a need for self-empowerment by talking about their many achievements. Yet we often brand them as self-centered and make sure not to get too involved.
- We might avoid someone we perceive as angry when the root of anger is fear. Fear can be of something apparently simple, but it has at its base a need for survival.

While people often act to get needs met and don't always get the results they were hoping for, we don't need to criticize and label them as difficult, since we now know that whatever they do, they do it because they think it will fulfill their needs. Dr. Glasser tells the story of a man arriving at a hotel in Arizona. As the doors opened on the shuttle bus, he jumped to the ground, tore off all his clothes and ran over to a cactus, rolling on it. Asked why, he said, "It seemed like a good idea at the time."

How we behave, whatever we do, even if we don't know Choice Theory, is based on the hope that our behavior will meet one or more particular needs—and it always seems like a good idea at the time. Dr. Glasser said that we do what feels like the right choice at the time.

Describing behavior in concrete terms is thus simplified. No longer do we need to spend time guessing at or labeling people's motivations. Their motivations are their business. We know their behavior is attempting to meet a need.

When we have a conversation with the difficult person and describe their behavior and the impact of their behavior, they will hopefully understand that a different behavior, without the negative impact, will also meet their needs. It is their motivation, and their decision.

Exercise One

1. Identify what you think is the negative behavior of your difficult person. Write it all down, all the complaints and irritations.
2. Examine the items on your list to see if what you have written is really a behavior or if it is a judgment. Is it an action that a person does or words that the person says? Make sure it is not your emotional reaction to the behavior but the behavior itself.
3. See if you can find ways to describe the behavior in a positive way. Someone who interrupts all the time is someone eager to understand. A child who doesn't immediately respond to a request could be a "creative dreamer." If we can look at "oppositional" as passion, and "argumentative" as hunting for answers, it is more possible to describe behavior without the emotional bite. If you can describe the specific behavior in a more positive way, chances are you are really describing behavior.
4. What understandable motivation could be driving the behavior of your difficult person?

CHAPTER FIVE

Impact, baby, impact

Defining Impact

In daring to dialogue with a difficult person, we not only have to describe the behavior we find irritating, but we also have to identify the impact of the behavior. If the difficult person isn't aware of the behavior, then they probably aren't aware of its impact. The impact can be on the other people in the difficult person's life, like family members, colleagues, customers, clients, and volunteers, or it can be on the difficult person themselves.

I had a colleague, Marie, with whom I had studied to become certified in Reality Therapy and with whom I later presented the material to a variety of students. One evening after we had been teaching, she invited me to have a drink with her. As we visited, she explained that she didn't think as rapidly as I did and I sometimes made her nervous. She said, "When you say things so quickly, so confidently, it makes me feel inadequate and stupid. I am so much slower than you. You make me all scared inside."

I was not particularly sympathetic. A core concept of the material we were teaching was that we choose our behaviors, which include actions that lead to our thoughts and feelings and impact our physiology. Everything is a choice, however subtle. Consequently, nobody can make anybody feel anything. Looking back, I realize that she was trying to share the impact of my behavior with me, but I heard only that I made her feel a certain way.

Despite my reaction to her you may want to identify a feeling to express to your difficult person. Saying we feel concerned, hurt, scared, or confused to the difficult person may be helpful to begin the conversation. In fact, it is natural and usually true. But to be really heard, we have to follow up our concern with a description of the behavior and its impact, without a judgment.

I believe I lost patience with her. Part of her personal style was to talk as if she were a little girl and most people found it endearing. I endured it. I remember feeling defensive because she kept saying I made her feel intimidated and I knew I couldn't make anybody feel anything. I have since learned that when I get defensive, it is because I am not really listening, and I need to stop taking it personally. I wish I had been able to hear her better.

I was unable to give credibility to her description of impact because it assigned a judgment to me. Her description of my behavior was that I was thinking and acting too fast for her, and her description of my impact was that I made her feel intimidated. Marie's judgment of us was that I was a powerhouse who knew everything and that she was stupid and slow. She was an experienced professional, at least ten years older than I, with incredible knowledge and experience. I was honestly puzzled.

In retrospect I now realize that the real impact on her was that the students might not perceive her as knowledgeable; it could damage her credibility. Maybe I would have heard her more clearly if she had said that. I don't know if I would have changed, but I know I would have immediately reassured her of her authority; she certainly had my respect. And maybe I would have attempted to watch how I was leading and how she was leading, and if I could see my leadership impinging on hers. I don't know.

The impact on us, the consequence, was that we grew apart. We worked together less, and our friendship dwindled. She didn't say, "If you keep doing this we can't work together," but that is what occurred.

In contrast, Denise's description of the behavior and its impact was clear and concise. She didn't explicitly say, "The consequence of not changing is that you may need to find another job," but I certainly understood the implication.

Part of the unwitting impact of the difficult person is the impression they give off. It can be just as important to communicate how we see them as it is to communicate the behavior and impact.

With Marie, it seemed absurd to me that I was intimidating because I wasn't aware of the impression I portrayed. It was only years later that I began to realize that my physical stance, my voice, and how I present myself make me appear confident and capable.

I still remember the very first time I stood in front a classroom of seventh graders in Providence, Rhode Island, and asked them to open their Ancient History books to page forty-two, and they did. I was amazed. I felt a chemical change in my body. I remember thinking, "Wow! It worked." I had been quaking in my boots.

Denise's impression of me was that I was completely unaware of my behavior, and she was right. There was no judgment involved.

My conclusion is that difficult people are unaware of the impression others have of them. Or if they have a hint of the judgments they are puzzled. Often part of why they don't know what they are doing, nor the impact, is because they don't know how others see them.

One woman who was a model for clearly communicating impact was a professional colleague in the non-profit world, Diane. She presented to a group of which I was a member and afterward shared privately with me that she was confused. She asked me why I had posed so many questions during her talk. I explained that I lived in the community where she was working, and I had an intense interest in all she had done. She said that it was clear that I knew a lot about the community and pointed out that my asking so many questions had begun to feel threatening to her. I was surprised and apologized, explaining that I was intensely curious about the topic and meant nothing negative. She said that with so many other people at the meeting, my questions began to feel as if I were suggesting she wasn't doing a good job. I assured her that that was the last thing I wanted to do.

I had intended my questions to show interest and support for her work, yet she began to feel judged. I was surprised and thanked her for telling me. I mentally vowed to make my questions more helpful and less spontaneous at any future presentations, not just hers.

More noteworthy to me was a week later, I experienced someone asking me numerous questions at a presentation. I could feel the hair on the back of my neck prickling, and I realized I was feeling defensive. It was an "ah-ha" moment. I thought, "That's what Diane must have felt." I wasn't really fearful that this individual doubted my expertise, although I was a little tired of getting countless questions from one person. I chose to applaud the questioner's interest in the topic and thank her for the questions. Since interest was what motivated my questions of Diane, I chose to believe that the same was true for my interrogator.

The difference between the way Marie talked to me and the way Diane talked to me is that both Marie's description of my behavior and its impact were judgmental of both her and me. Diane described my behavior and asked why I did it. She shared the behavior and its impact. Then she asked, "Is this what you intended?"

And of course, it wasn't.

45

Diane was able to describe the behavior and how she was feeling, but she didn't say I "made her feel" that way. She said she felt a certain way based on her reaction to my behavior of asking copious questions. Her reaction was based on her impression of me and her judgment about that impression. She didn't say, "Your examination felt like you think you know more than I do." She could have. She would not have been alone in that thought. I later learned that others had that impression of me and made negative judgments about me based on that impression.

To have a conversation with a difficult person, it is important to identify the behavior, the impact on others, and the impression we have of the difficult person—all without judgment.

Is It Worth It?

Defining the impact of the behavior can clarify whether the effort to have the conversation is worth it. The impact could be a loss of your relationship with the difficult person or negative effects on you from the difficult behavior itself. The importance of your connection to the difficult person will dictate whether you want to continue preparing for a conversation. You will want to share your motivations with your difficult person by explaining the value of the relationship and how it is affected by the behavior.

Articulate why the relationship is important. We all want to feel that we belong and that others want us around. A difficult person needs to know that you value a relationship with them enough to have a conversation with them. Denise told me that she admired my work and wanted to continue training with me. Diane and I had always had a positive working relationship, and we continued to do so. I heard Marie's comments as criticism and resisted her comments, mentally scratching my head. That relationship floundered.

In a work situation, it is probably something along the lines of the quality of their work, but it can also be to preserve the personal relationship. I held a job in sales for a few months where I was told that my work ethic was terrific and my boss would like all his staff to work as hard as I did. He had to let me go because I wasn't selling, but he retrained me twice because he wanted me to succeed. I wasn't designed for sales, but I am still friends with that boss.

In a family or friendship, the value is in the relationship. Sincere comments like, "I admire you," "I love you," or "I want to keep our friendship," are reassuring. Since the difficult person doesn't know what they are doing, the information that it creates a problem usually has a negative reaction. In addition to explaining the impact, it is vital to remind the difficult person that we are having the conversation because we care about them and we want to maintain the work/family/friend relationship. If we are able to include this in the conversation, we create a dynamic where the difficult person is encouraged to amend their behavior to meet their need for belonging.

Knowing the impact of my behavior and that my colleagues valued me made it easier for me to stop. After the conversation with Diane, I tried to tone down my questions in meetings. I also attempted to self-evaluate before I asked a question to see if I was merely being argumentative. When I found myself feeling "passionate" about a topic, I checked to see if I was having a tantrum.

When we dare to ask the difficult person if the behavior is intentional and then ask if they want to create a certain impact, we are inviting the person to make the choice to change or not. Just as you had the choice to determine whether the impact was worth having the conversation, the difficult person also has a choice on whether the impact is worth changing their behavior. In a world where people act as if they can "make" another change, I am advocating respect for the other person's freedom of choice.

Dr. Glasser teaches us that we are internally motivated to act and change to meet our internal needs. Being given a choice fulfills the need for freedom. When we ask our difficult person if they know they are doing the behavior and if they intend the impact, we are giving them the opportunity to be responsible for their own behavior.

Initially, a difficult person may blame their behavior on another person. The response is to remain calm in repeating that this behavior has created this impact and potential consequences. Then we can ask if that is what they want. Nobody wakes up in the morning dreaming of how to be difficult.

Some professionals tell me that some difficult people just don't want to change and no amount of explaining, describing, negotiating, threatening or imploring has led to a desire to change. My conclusion is that, in those cases, the consequences of not changing do not outweigh the benefits of acting as they do. There may be people like this in your life, but my experience is that people who discover that others find them "difficult" are usually interested in understanding and changing.

Jim's Story

Consider this example of Jim, the boss, who has invited Tom, a difficult yet valued employee, into a meeting.

J: Tom, I asked you to come in this morning because I have something important to talk to you about. But to start with, do you have anything for me?

T: Well I'm annoyed that you pulled me in when we are so busy, but that is nothing new. You're always dragging us into something we don't need. What do you want?

J: Gee, Tom it's interesting that you should make those comments to me today, kind of implying that you are too busy and my ideas aren't very important. Do you know that you do that a lot?

T: Me? Hah! You're too thin-skinned. That's just my way. Pay it no mind.

J: Well, Tom, I am paying it some mind because I don't think you are aware of how many times you say something critical about me or about the company. You do it a lot, do you know that?

T: Well, pay it no mind, I don't mean anything by it.

J: I am paying it some mind, Tom, because it impacts all of us and especially the new guys when you consistently put down the boss of the company and me. I am not taking it personally. But when you are negative over and over, with your seniority it has some influence. I believe it impacts newer employees so they think they have permission to complain. They think it is the right way to work here. Did you know you have that kind of influence?

T: Well, sure I know they follow me 'cause I am their trainer, but hey, it's my personality to be cutting away at other people; it's just my way.

J: So you know you do it? You're aware of it?

T: Listen, my father worked here before you were born and he was just the same way. My personality has no bearing on how I get the job done.

J: I hear you feeling a little defensive, Tom. This is not an attack. I want to make sure you understand what I'm saying. Your negativity spills over and implies to new hires that they can be critical too. It spills over when you talk to customers, and you are doing that more and more. And it spills over and makes it harder to work with you. Is that what you want?

T: Good lord. You make me sound like a giant spiller—I am just me, doing my job. How come you never complained before?

J: Because we didn't have all these new hires before. With our new way of doing business and more productivity, we touch the customers more, and it will hurt sales if our staff has a negative attitude.

T: Jeez Louise—what's the big deal?

J: Tom, you have a lot of influence here, I respect you and want to keep working with you. Do you understand the consequences of staying negative?

T: Shit, now you're gonna fire me because I am not Mr. "All-Sweetness-and-Light"? For God's sake, what is this world coming to? You aren't always positive either, you know.

J: Yes, I DO know that, Tom. I am noticing it in me and in you. I am trying to catch it in myself, and I am asking if you will do the same.

T: For God's sake—I need to remake my personality now? What on earth am I gonna say? This is beyond weird. This is crazy.

J: You sound frustrated Tom.

T: Well, jeez, you want me to be a different person.

J: No, I don't. I want all of your experience and teaching skill and ability to figure out what the customer needs. The problem is the offhand negative comments, like what you said when you came in here today, that start turning off the customers and sneaking into the attitudes of the new hires. Do you remember what you said?

T: Nope.

J: Well you said that you didn't know why I'd pull you in when we're so busy. This implies that I am getting in your way of doing your job and I must be a pretty stupid person to do that.

T: It does? I was just annoyed because we have that new big order and I am afraid the newbies will get it all wrong and I'll have to do it over again. Waste of my time.

J: I know you were annoyed—that's fair—but do you see how that comment implies that I am a bad boss? That if you say it out in the shop, the newbies think it is an okay attitude?

T: Yeah okay—course you are a bad boss, boss (laughs). Nah, just fooling. So that's what you want me to change?

J: Well, Tom, the fact is I can't have people working here spreading negativity. What do you think will happen if you keep doing it?

T: I get it, sheesh. I don't know if I can talk at all now—what else did I say?

J: You said I am always coming up with something that takes time but doesn't get the job done—again a suggestion that maybe my ideas aren't as important as the work you are doing.

T: Well, the point is to produce and sell, right? But yeah, I get it.

J: You're right—the point *is* to produce and sell and you do it really well. And when we were smaller, I could overlook your attitude. But you are touching more customers now and, more importantly, you are training others who will work here after you and I leave. We need them to respect the company, and that means less negativity. Okay?

T: Sheesh—I guess so. Don't know what I'm gonna say.

J: If it isn't too silly, what if you tried this? A rubber band on your wrist—and every time you hear yourself complain, you snap yourself. Whaddya think?

T: Stupid, but I'll try it.

J: Thanks, Tom. Maybe we need a signal that I could give you if I hear you being negative. Would that work?

T: Okay, what about pulling your ear?

J: And if you don't like it, let's talk some more. Do you want to get a handle on how much complaining you do?

T: Yeah, I guess so.

J: Let me know what you decide to do—I'll catch you sometime next week, okay? And keep up the good work.

This was a role play where I played Jim, and Jim played the role of Tom. Jim had originally attended the workshop to figure out how to fire Tom. As he defined the behavior and identified the impact, it made the issue less of a personal situation. He had respect for Tom's experience and was relieved to have an alternative to firing Tom. He feared Tom's negative reaction to being told his behavior had negative consequences.

Note that, despite his many dismissals, I persisted in asking if Tom knew he did the behavior and if he wanted that impact. As Jim, I acknowledged that I wasn't perfect either and that I was trying to remain positive in a time of change at the company. I even suggested a method for Tom to become more aware of his behavior.

You may think the conversation seemed to drag on, but it is likely that you will need to endure a certain amount of "dragging on" in your real conversation.

Jim told me that, after this role play, he had more confidence in himself in the conversation. It was a little scary, but they got through it, and Tom appeared to be watching his negativity. Now all Jim had to do was say something like, "Love the attitude of the new hires, don't you?" when Tom seemed to be particularly grumpy. Jim reported that Tom didn't turn into Pollyanna, but his negativity greatly diminished and he was not fired. That made everybody happy.

Exercise Two

Taking the personal judgment out of our definition of behavior, identifying its impact, expressing our impression of the difficult person, and articulating the value of the relationship all take practice.

1. Write a statement about the impact of the behavior. Be as specific as possible. The behavior may have an impact on you personally, on your clients, your family members, a larger organization or community. This impact needs to be described without judgment and bias so that the difficult person can understand it. Denise said to me, "You are raising the anxiety level for all of us." She reported how my behavior touched the rest of the staff without a negative judgment.

2. Write a statement describing the potential consequences if the behavior continues. My inability to hear Marie's description of my behavior and its impact had the consequence of a gradual ending of our friendship.

3. Write a statement about your impression of the difficult person. Can you describe your impression without judging them?
4. Write down three reasons it's worth it for you to have the conversation with the person because of their value. What do you like, appreciate, respect, admire, or cherish about the person? Be as specific about this as possible, as concrete as you are about their behavior.

You now have a good start in identifying what you want to say to your difficult person.

CHAPTER SIX

WHAT EMOTIONS GET IN THE WAY?

Avoidance

B eing able to describe the behavior and the impact is obviously not an easy task, which is why it requires practice. We do it in the workshop, and you can do it on your own. If it were as simple as identifying the pieces of what you want to say, more people would be doing it, and more people would have done it with me.

In the course of my research, I became more aware of the ways people had indirectly tried to get through to me. My performance reviews usually included a need for improved communication skills, which confused me. I just smiled and said, "Okay." At one organization, I would receive a flier in my mailbox at work a few times a year, announcing a workshop for "Dealing with Difficult People," or "Managing Conflict in the Workplace," and again I was confused. I wasn't the training manager but I provided a good deal of training to the non-profit community, so I figured someone was sharing the fliers with me to share them with others. I have now concluded that sharing the fliers was the only way someone could find to tell me there was a problem. Such is the power of avoidance.

I have made a point of studying the extent to which people avoid the process. People tell me that they dodge having the conversation with a difficult person because they don't know what to say. The good news is that *now we know how*. We can describe the behavior in terms of what the person says or does, identify the impact of the behavior, articulate our impression of the difficult person, and share with them why they are important to us. If you have been doing the suggested written work, you actually have the statements written down.

That should make it simple, right?

Well, not always.

Another cause for hesitation about approaching the difficult person is that we fear their reaction. You are not alone in fearing having the conversation.

We have to stop at this point and look at ourselves. It is natural and common to want to avoid conflict because of fear. One way to overcome fear is to gain insights into what is causing the fear, and how to improve the chance of resolution through conversation.

Are There Difficult People in Your Past?

If something bothers me about another person, and I am afraid of angering them, I have learned to ask myself, *"Who do they remind me of?"*

In my case, anybody in authority reminded me of my older sister, Regina, or my mother. That meant none of them were to be trusted. I believed that to survive I had to argue with them and have opinions about their actions and decisions. When I was in charge of my own classroom it wasn't a problem—I was the authority. But as a member of a faculty team or work team, it was labeled "difficult." It took me a long time to understand that those with authority over me were not members of my family deserving distrust.

As another example, Marie's demeanor annoyed me because it reminded me of my childhood piano teacher, Mrs. Fisk. She was an extremely frail woman who would pick me up from school and drive me to her house for my lesson until my mother picked me up. She whistled between her teeth when driving the car and she called me "Say-rah." It felt like an alien pronunciation, and as if she didn't really see me. It made me uncomfortable, and I didn't like her. I thought the piano music was boring and I didn't practice very often. I particularly hated her when she would say, "Now come on, dearie. I have a third grader who can play better than that." She always said it jokingly, and I'm sure she thought it was a good way to motivate me, but it truly backfired. I wanted to say, "Then go play with the third grader; this is who I am. I don't want to play for you."

I realized that Marie had some of the same characteristics of Mrs. Fisk: a little fussy, an emphasis on the feminine, and a way of presenting herself as if she didn't know something when she actually knew it well. Although I was probably more of a difficult person for Marie than she was for me, I did become annoyed at her self-effacing style. I expect that explains some of why I wasn't able to hear Marie's comments as a cry for help, and I wish I had realized it at the time. It never occurred to me that Marie was uncomfortable.

I needed to acknowledge that they were not the same person, and write out how they were different. When contrasting Marie with Mrs. Fisk, I found Mrs. Fisk to be overly picky, unfriendly, critical, and timid. Marie was full of energy and enthusiasm for me and her students. She had been helpful when we studied together, and she liked meeting new people and going to new places—the opposite of timid.

It may surprise you to see how you, yourself, have changed since you last interacted with the person from your past. Some of the ways I have changed since the conversation with Marie include my new reaction when someone says, "You make me feel..." I no longer immediately say, "I can't make you feel anything." I have learned to say to myself, "Listen and learn," and then to the other person, "I'm sorry you feel that way." I remember that the feeling is real to them and I ask about what caused it. I try to be a listener and not someone with all the answers. I have discovered that my tone of voice can be irritating and I am still learning to modify that.

It helps to identify what you liked about the difficult person. I envied Marie's ability to laugh at herself and her joy in life. She was friendly, warm and encouraging. She was smart and had great teaching ideas, and I admired her relationships with her students.

It would have been helpful if I had done this exercise when I was teaching with Marie. Doing this now has changed the way I remember her, and if she were in my life today, I would apologize.

Exercise Three

1. As you reflect on your difficult person, write the answer to the question: "Who do they remind me of? How? And what is my instant reaction to that person?"
2. List all the ways they are NOT the same as the person from the past.
3. List how you are different today than how you were with the person in the past.
4. Take the time to list the positive qualities that make your difficult person different from the one from your past. Then put a star next to the top three qualities you appreciate about them.

Fact or Feeling?

"Being resentful, they say, is like taking poison and
waiting for the other person to die."
- Alan Brandt

When we are upset, we can get confused between facts and feelings, blaming the other person. Having the conversation with a difficult person probably won't work unless we can see the difference between our feelings and the facts. Sometimes we have held on to our irritation for a long time, and it can become resentment. Resentment is the silent killer. We can sometimes find these feelings overpowering.

Dr. Glasser says that our feelings are part of our behavioral system, second to thoughts and linked inextricably with our actions and our physiology. Dr. Gordon says that it is impossible for someone to hear the facts unless their feelings are acknowledged and accepted first. His skill at working with teenagers includes his acceptance of both the individuals themselves and their feelings, whatever the feelings were. In his parenting classes, he taught mothers and fathers to listen to their children's feelings before trying to employ logic or facts.

In my past, feelings were facts. I believed that they were as real as the sky is blue. It has taken some wise, patient people to help me understand that my feelings are just feelings, period. When supervisors requested corrections, I heard criticism. I felt, "Something is wrong with me." It always brought tears. I got very angry at myself because no matter how hard I tried, I couldn't accept correction without tears. I confused the correction with my sister Regina's message from my childhood that there was something wrong with me. The correction might have to do with how I related to others or the quality of my work, but I always heard that there was something wrong with me, and it triggered despair.

My supervisors would acknowledge my tears and point out that they were not criticizing me; they wanted a better quality of work. No one ever said, "There's something wrong with you." It was my own internal message. My feeling. Not a fact.

The tears were harder to stop when I sensed an injustice. One particular example stands out from my time working with volunteers. Tom, a colleague who managed volunteers in a different program, was invited to take the management training offered by our national company. I asked my supervisor if I could attend the training too. She checked and was told that my job did not require it so I wasn't eligible.

I was perplexed. Tom and I had the same title. I not only managed an entire volunteer program, but I also taught other paid staff of non-profits how to manage volunteer programs. I expressed a sense of righteous indignation, which I have since learned is a perfect way to be labeled "difficult." How could I not benefit from the management training offered by our national organization? My supervisor encouraged me to talk to the vice president.

I made an appointment and explained my position. The VP told me that the caliber of volunteers that Tom was managing was different because they were from professions like manufacturing, law, banking, and marketing. I responded that the volunteers that I managed were from a variety of backgrounds, many of them retired professionals. In addition, I interacted with professionals at City Hall where the volunteers worked, often including the mayor, the city manager, and city councilmembers. I am sure there was hostility in my tone because it was clear to me the man didn't know anything about my job.

In hindsight, I realize now that the company was grooming Tom for management. However, it felt sexist to me, and I ended up right there in raging tears in the VP's office. I remember the look of puzzlement on his face, as if thinking, "Yikes, now what do I do?"

How frustrating as a woman to be crying right in the middle of battling sexism.

I apologized for the tears, saying, "Just because I am crying doesn't mean my facts are incorrect. You are giving Tom special treatment, and I have been here as long as he has, and I am doing the same job. I work with as many professional people as he does. Not only that, the other half of my job is training others in management skills and the other half of Tom's job is an administrative assistant. I have more responsibility than he does. I don't think it is fair that he qualifies for the training and I don't."

There I stood with tears running down my face because I felt I had to stand up for myself. I wasn't able to distinguish between feelings and facts because, when the facts seemed to say I was being discriminated against, I plopped immediately into feelings. They were very familiar, from my childhood, and I blamed the other person for my pain.

The VP actually agreed with me. He said that he hadn't realized what my work entailed. This is a common experience for people who manage volunteer programs, but this was the first time I had met it so forcefully. It led me to a career of advocating for managers of volunteer programs, and this had been my first awkward attempt. I grew more skillful, but on that occasion I cried because I was arguing with the boss, triggering my internal belief from childhood that another authority was out to get me.

When he finally did agree with me and told me I could attend the training, I found it hard to stop crying. After thanking him for changing his mind, I then asked him if he would please tell me a joke so I could leave his office laughing. Again, a look of confusion and almost desperation crossed his face. I recall finding that humorous and telling a few jokes myself. We laughed, and he finally thought of a joke so that when I left the office I was no longer seething with hostility and crying.

Difficult people often confuse facts and feelings, and when we are dealing with difficult people, we need to ask ourselves if we are doing the same thing. If the difficult person reminds us of someone from our past who hurt us, then the feelings we have for the person in front of us need to be examined through that lens. We also need to ask ourselves if we are having a feeling that has little to do with the actual facts. Then we need to examine the facts from *outside* of that lens.

Exercise Four

1. Make a list of the feelings that you have about the difficult person. There is a good chance that resentment is on the list, as well as anger and fear. Note how many of them come from the person of whom you are reminded.
2. Now look back at the list of the actual behaviors, and their impact. What are really the facts?
3. Make a list of only the feelings that you have about the facts of the impact. There may be frustration that the difficult person is doing something, sadness that the relationship is changing, concern that the difficult person is creating the impact, and so on. These are the here-and-now feelings based on the facts, not the feelings from the past.

These feelings are the ones to mention in your conversation.

Jason's Story

Here is a dialogue with the angry person we all fear. Jason calls his difficult older brother, Bill:

J: Bill, how much longer is mom and dad's will going to be in probate? It's been more than a year.

B: If that's the only reason you are calling, I'm hanging up. I am not going to talk about this.

J: Bill, have a heart, I'm your brother. They left the money to both of us. I'm just curious. Are you ok? What's going on?

B: Jason, you're a wastrel, and they should have known better than to leave you anything that isn't in a trust. My mind is made up about this, and if you don't stop asking me about it, I will hang up and never talk to you again. *(voice rising)*

J: Bill, you sound so defensive, please, don't hang up. Please don't hang up.

B: I'm not defensive; I'm pissed. I'm the executor, and I will tell you when the money is available.

J: Before I die, Bill? We aren't either of us getting any younger, haha.

B: Don't be rude, you brat.

J: All right, sorry—but jeepers, why do you sound so angry with me?

B: You know why. You don't have a real job, and you don't take care of yourself, you live on the beach, for goodness sake, and I just know you will blow all the money.

J: Yeah, I know I don't live up to your picture of a mature individual, and you think my college education is wasted, I get it. But Bill, why does that matter? You took care of me all the time while we were growing up. You're a great older brother, but did you expect me to be just like you?

B: I don't know what you are talking about and this is a dumb conversation. I am hanging...

J: Bill, I miss you. I miss our friendship. Don't hang up, Bill, please—I am really serious. I want to work this out with you, and I'd really like to do it as if we were the friends we used to be.

B: Oh for goodness sake, this is silly.

J: Bill, you're co-executor with the bank, I know that. You really can't keep that money forever. Can you? Right now you hang up on me and don't return my calls, and I feel blocked. I can't believe you really want me to go to a lawyer, do you?

B: A lawyer? *(voice rising)* NOW I AM...

J: BILL. NO, NO, DON'T HANG UP. You sound so angry and defensive. Talk to me. Do you see how your behavior would lead me to go that way? I hear you being super critical of me—I am not critical of you, bro. I want to know why. This isn't the way you used to be.

B: You have no idea of the responsibility this is—all the 't's that have to be crossed, and the 'i's that have to be dotted, and all the rules and regulations, and there's never anything simple about it. It's all, file this and wait, then file this and wait. And the banker says it just takes time and not to worry, but I don't know if we are really doing it right. I have read three books on this now, and I still don't think I totally understand it. I'm not a lawyer or a banker, I'm just a teacher, and this is giving me heartburn, and I think I am getting an ulcer.

J: Wow. *(Silence)* Bill, this sounds horrible. Do you realize that this is the first time you told me this? I had no idea. What does Natalie think?

B: She thinks I should just let the banker do what he's doing and stop worrying about it. She has been hassling me about this 'cause I don't want to do anything with the kids anymore. I am so tired when I get home every day; our life isn't much fun. We argue about it a lot.

J: Jeez, Bill. Why don't you all pack up and come to the beach for a weekend—spend some time with Uncle Jason?

B: Now is not the time to play, Jason, this is too serious. See, there you go again, being irresponsible.

J: Bill, would it help you if you knew that I have been part owner of the surf shop for six months now, and I'm earning a real salary? I actually have had some ideas that increased our sales, and we're growing and expanding. It would be fun to show it off to you and the boys—Natalie could use a break at the beach, right? If I found you a place to stay, can you get them over here to Hawaii?

B: Oh, Jason, I don't know.

J: Well, think about it…and could you ask the banker if we could have any of the money? Maybe you could pay for your trip that way?

B: You're irresponsible, Jason. The money is for college for the boys.

J: Sure, I know, but there's also enough for one family holiday to Hawaii. I hate to think of you sitting in wine country in California, having heartburn and not enjoying life. It was different when I thought you had just turned into a conservative old curmudgeon, but I hear the brother I used to know under all that stress. Whaddya say?

B: Well, I'll think about it. I'll talk to Natalie and the banker, and we'll talk again soon—okay?

J: Great.

This was actually the first of three conversations that Jason had with his brother before the family finally took a vacation.

Jason had personified his brother as a miserly, negative, conservative, distrustful old man at the beginning of the workshop. As we went through the process and Jason did his self-reflection work, he realized it wasn't like his brother and began to wonder what was going on. He began to wonder if it was fact or his feeling. Their childhood relationship had been a good one, and it seemed that since their parents had died, Bill had somehow changed. He was always one to follow the rules while Jason hadn't, but it had never before caused this great a rift.

Because of the work Jason had done about his feelings, he could focus on how he valued his brother and wanted to find out what was troubling him.

When we role-played in the workshop, Jason played his brother, and I was Jason. Bill didn't identify the heartburn, but he did acknowledge that the whole experience was stressful. When I, as Jason, suggested that the consequence of the time lag was that I might get a lawyer, in the role-play Bill hung up. So we determined that it was not something to say in quite such forceful terms when he made the real call. We tried again and I, as Jason, focused on wanting a real relationship.

Jason had to find a way to describe the behavior in nonjudgmental terms and the impact on him. Beyond being angry, he realized that he was curious and sad about their relationship changing so much. Because he had examined this and done some practice, he was able to articulate that in the real calls.

CHAPTER SEVEN

ARE YOU IN YOUR OWN WAY?

Whose Business Am I In?

Byron Katie, founder of The Work, teaches that to be at peace in life it is important to stay in our own business. She means that we need to pay attention to what is about us and consider only what is about us. She identifies three kinds of business:

1. our business, which has to do with us, the individual person,
2. the others' business, which is a person other than us, the individual person, and
3. God's business, which is everything else.

As you look at the difficult person, I encourage you to ask yourself: "Am I in their business, my business, or God's business?"

Most difficult people have the annoying habit of being in another person's business. I believe that this is one ever-available way to have the feeling of being in control. I think I have tried to control what is outside of me because I wasn't sure I could control what was inside. One of my irritating routines when in other people's business, is feeling compelled to answer questions that were not asked of me and remind people of what they said, when not asked.

This example comes from a staff meeting in a job I held at my church. We were a compatible and cheerful group, and we grew very close after going through some challenging times. One member was hard of hearing, and when he asked a question, many of us would respond. He requested that only the chair of the meeting answer and most of us were able to do that. I, being me, often forgot and he had to remind me. I did eventually learn, but it reminded me of another colleague who used to rage at me because I finished his sentences for him. He felt disrespected, and he was right. When he mentioned it, I was always startled that I had done it again, and then accepted his request and pledged to stop. But I found stopping difficult. Something in me feels compelled to finish the sentence, answer the question, and thus, be in charge. I believe it is partially speaking my thoughts without thinking and partially a reaction to the tension at home as a child. I found it useful to know who was saying what, who was going where, and when. It helped me feel safe. Even now, I still catch myself doing it. Once again the world labels this interfering behavior as "difficult."

I have often been in someone else's business. In 1981, I was certified in the practice and teaching of Reality Therapy and was invited to assist as a teacher. The professor who led the training, Dr. Bob Wubbolding, has become a personal friend and a man I very much admire and respect. I was thrilled to be assisting him in training his participants, along with other certified instructors. Bob met with us early each day to go over the agenda and assure himself that we knew what to do in our small groups. On the first day, we instructors observed as Bob completed his session and reviewed the schedule. I noticed that he had changed the times on our agenda and raised my hand. I pointed out that his original agenda had been different and asked if he was sure of the timing just described. He smiled and said. "Oh, yes, I've changed my mind. Thanks for noticing."

One of my friends in the instructor group turned to me and said with a big smile, "You really are a controlling bitch, aren't you?" I realized that he meant it as a joke and the other instructors laughed, but I also heard it as a criticism. I was confused and hurt. Didn't Bob want to stick to his schedule? Wouldn't he want to know if he had left something out? Because I was worrying about what Bob was doing and what would happen if he didn't do what he had told the instructors he was going to do, I thought it was important to correct him, or at least check.

I was completely doing his job as if I were the boss. I was in his business. This kind of behavior, even among friends, was obviously what some folks call "difficult." I was blessed that Bob was a pro and a deep respecter of differences and didn't indicate that it bothered him at all that I had asked. I never did it again. It wasn't my business.

I now view people who appear anxious about event timing and changes as possibly people like me who like to know everything because it helps them feel a sense of control over their world. I tell myself that they are not difficult, they are concerned. I try to respond with compassion for their concern, thank them and invite them to allow life to unfold. I admit that allowing life to unfold is still challenging for me.

A helpful illustration of how to gently correct difficult people who are in your business occurred when I was co-leading a week-long personal growth workshop in Illinois with my mentor, Dr. Sidney B. Simon. It was an exhilarating opportunity for me, and I was elated to be there. I wanted to teach well, have fun, and do the right things so he would invite me to lead with him again. At one point, when he was leading a session and I was part of the group, he taught a concept, and I realized that he had left out a piece. Not thinking of anything but the fact that he must have forgotten and that it was important that everybody learn the information, I raised my hand and reminded him. He was very smooth and thanked me for it, restated it, and then invited us to journal about it and share with our partners.

While the group got busy, Sid walked over to me quietly, kneeled down, and whispered, "Thanks for the reminder. I might not have remembered, but when I am leading you get to relax and let me decide what I will share." There was no hint of negative criticism in his voice; it was a loving message to let him do his thing and that I didn't need to take care of him. I had been acting as if I knew what was best for him by deciding he needed to be corrected. But he didn't say any of that explicitly.

After he had walked away, I looked at my partner, looked at my notebook where I had been writing, and burst into tears. I had screwed up, I had been controlling and intrusive, I was a failure as a co-leader, and he would never ask me back. My partner asked me, "What did that remind you of? What authority in your childhood does Sid represent for you?" I realized that it was my mother and older sister who, in my memory, only criticized my behavior. I acknowledged that Sid wasn't my mother or my older sister. As I cried and began to list how Sid wasn't like the critical people in my life, my tears dried up. I could see that he had been as loving as anybody could be. I could see that I was trying to do his job. I was in his business. The issue passed.

I learned not to interrupt my co-leader. And Sid invited me to co-lead with him again many times.

In the examples above, I was in other people's business because I thought I had to know all the answers. It made me feel more in control when I had the answers. The fact that I felt compelled to share them made me unpopular and got me labeled "controlling." Although these two professionals handled my interference well, many of us find this kind of meddling quite annoying and "difficult."

To understand more about being in our own business, let's refer back to some previous stories. My wonderful supervising teacher, Dorothy, was completely in my business when she chose not to tell me that my behavior was perceived as argumentative and negative. She applauded my quick thinking and my passion, and she had a sister like me, so she was comfortable with this behavior. She decided it was in my best interest to let me do my work and simply point out to her boss that I was exceptionally good at my job.

She was correct that it would have hurt my feelings a good deal to know what the principal thought of me. Yet, she was taking responsibility for my feelings. She was in my business. In the long run, partly because of her decision, I developed a reputation for being difficult to work with and was not given the feedback I needed in order to choose for myself. I didn't change until years later when Denise told me that my behavior had a negative impact.

When we think we know why someone is doing something, how they will react, and how to make it better for them, we are putting ourselves in the middle of their business. Some people call this having no boundaries.

Counselors call it enmeshment. Sounds a little scary, doesn't it? Like a spider web.

It takes a good deal of energy and only brings heartache because being in someone else's business becomes manipulation, and nobody likes to be manipulated. When we are in another person's business, we think we are being helpful and put forth lots of effort only to receive anger from the other. Then we then feel as if they are ungrateful. The other person doesn't change, and we are frustrated. We sincerely believe we are doing it out of the kindness of our hearts and it leads to great pain for all concerned.

As another example, I was in Marie's business when I argued with her feelings and her logic. I decided that it was my job to remind her about what we were teaching others. If I had been in my business, I hope I would have gone inside and checked, "Am I trying to intimidate Marie with my training efficiency? No," and I would have conveyed that to her. If I had been in my business, I would have asked what she wanted from me and then decided if I could give that to her. Instead, I embarked on an unsuccessful teaching lecture that frustrated us both.

If you think the difficult person should change to be a "better person," or that you need to teach them, it is probable that you are in their business. It is possible you are trying to make them different to make yourself feel better. Byron Katie points out that this is HOPELESS.

Being in another person's business is, in our world, a sneaky thing. Most of the programs on TV create humor and conflict because people get into each other's business. So we get trapped in another person's business or God's business without even seeing it. For more information on being in your own business, go to www.thework.com or Byron Katie's book, *Loving What Is*.

If the behavior of your difficult person has a specific negative effect on you, your team, your customers, your family, or a group for whom you are responsible, then you are probably in your own business. When Diane asked if I realized my questions during her presentation had the impact of making her uncomfortable, she wasn't in my business, she was in her own.

One of the reasons I love Dr. Glasser's Choice Theory and Reality Therapy is that he invites people to be responsible for their own behavior and to stay in their own business. His theory of motivation with the five basic needs that reflect genetic instructions allows us to stay in our own business. Why does someone do something? Because at the time, it is perceived to be need-fulfilling. Does it actually fulfill the target needs? Maybe or maybe not, but unless it impacts us, it's not our business.

If we have identified someone's behavior and its impact, clarified how they are different from a feared person from our past, distinguished between fact and feeling, and verified that we have a valid reason for talking to them—in other words, verified that it *is* our business— we have a more rational view of the difficult person and how to proceed.

Donna's Story

Donna is a first-year college student telephoning her overbearing mother.

S: So sweetie when are you coming home for the holidays?

D: Well, I'll come home a day before Christmas, but I am going skiing the day after Christmas with some friends. We'll go back to school from there.

S: You're just coming home for two days? But you get out of class so early after your exams—why aren't you coming home on the 18th or 19th?

D: Mom, I have so much work to finish up after I study for exams, and besides, some of my friends are staying around, and I want to be here with them.

S: So, is a boy involved?

D: Mom, it's none of your business.

S: Well, I pay the bills around here so it IS my business.

D: Mom, please? We've talked about this before. You pay my bills, I appreciate it, and I am getting good experience and good grades. I love you Mom, but you keep butting into my personal life—it's called personal for a reason, Mom.

S: That's just unacceptable.

D: Mom, please hear me. When you always want to know about my love life and meet every friend of mine and interview every boy I like, it wears me out and makes me not want to tell you anything. Can you see why I tell you less and less? You act like you're in charge of my life and I feel trapped.

S: You're such a baby. I just don't want you to get hurt.

D: I know Mom.

S: You know what happened to me and I don't want that to happen to you—you're only twenty years old and you have your whole life ahead of you.

D: I know Mom—I am sorry you had to leave school to get married and have me. But I wouldn't trade my childhood for anybody's, Mom. I am so grateful for all you have done, but you can't keep me under a glass jar. Smothering plants kills them; you know that, right?

S: I am not smothering.

D: Do you ask me about boys every time we talk? Do you?

S: No.

D: Yeah, Mom, (laughs) you do. Seriously, do you warn me not to get pregnant every time we talk?

S: No.

D: Yeah, Mom, you do.

S: Well, we hardly ever talk anymore.

D: See? It's hard to talk to you. You don't seem to care about my classes, you just want to know if I am dating some boy and maybe having sex. You ask me personal questions that you'd have hated your mother to ask, right? I love you, but it is so frustrating to talk to you anymore. Makes me not want to call or return your calls or texts.

S: Well, I care about your classes, but I guess I don't really understand them and it makes me feel bad that I didn't finish college myself.

D: Why don't you?

S: Why don't I what?

D: Finish college?

S: Oh for goodness sake—I'm way too old.

D: Nope—not true. I told you about this thirty-five-year-old man, a veteran, in my psych class, and there's a woman who is a grandmother in my French class, so she is older than you are. You're not too old.

S: Is this vet the man you are dating?

D: Mom! I'm not kidding…I am gonna hang up if you don't stop.

S: No, don't hang up. Please? I love you, that's all.

D: I love you too, Mom.

S: So, there's a grandmother in your French class? Hmm…I was pretty good in French.

D: Yeah, the prof was pretty excited when I sang that song you taught me when I was a kid. He praised my accent. See, you're pretty smart, for an old lady. (Laughs)

S: Well, I don't know about that, and I don't know about going back to college, but I guess that's why I always ask about boys.

D: Mom, there are boys here. Some of them are nice, and I go to the movies or study with them. I don't have a steady guy—I learned from you—now let's talk about you going to college, ok?

S: Well, will you come home earlier and stay longer if I don't ask about your love life?

D: Well, I will do my best to come home earlier. I have two papers to write before the 20th, the end of the semester. I'll tell you what. I'll do my research here and come home to write it. You can help me, like the old days. That'll help you see how smart you are. I can file them online. Okay?

S: That's a great plan. I'll try not to pry anymore.

D: I am still going skiing with some people the day after Christmas, but I'll ask them if they want to stay over that night, and we'll leave the next day— then you can get to know them a little and maybe stop worrying about me, okay?

Donna had to do a good deal of reflection and self-examination before she had this talk. When she reported this actual conversation, she said she was astonished by how there was only love in it. Notice that Donna never raised her voice to her mother or accused her of being a snoop and a meddler, which is how she originally described her to the workshop. She said normally she would have gotten angry with her mother when her mom said, "That's unacceptable." That kind of comment had driven Donna into rages and hooked her into telling her mother to go find someone else to bother. Donna saw that this reaction stemmed from feelings, not fact, and invaded her mother's business. Having done her work to be in her own business, she no longer felt angry about her mother's questions, and she said they were both in tears at the end of the call.

She reported that her mother is in school and loving it and now their conversations are about class work and Donna has a greater sense of privacy.

Lori's Story

Probably the toughest time to stay in your own business is when it involves family. Lori is married with three children between the ages of ten and twenty, and her husband's family lives nearby, a father and a sister. Traditionally, their holidays are celebrated with the in-laws, usually at the home of the sister-in-law. As Lori shared in the workshop, describing the behavior of her sister-in-law, Judith, I realized that Lori had issues both with her sister-in-law's behavior and her husband's unwillingness to acknowledge the problem.

When Judith drank alcohol, she became taunting and sarcastic to both Lori and her children. She mocked their achievements and made fun of their health challenges. Lori's children told their mom they didn't want to celebrate Christmas at Aunt Judith's this year. When Lori talked to her husband, he responded that he felt the kids and Lori were overreacting. He believed that Judith was no different at parties than at any other time.

Lori was confused about whose business she was in. She wanted to protect her children and herself from what she perceived was abuse, but she could only speak for herself. Her oldest daughter, Evelyn, had asked Aunt Judith not to drink when taking her out to dinner at college and her aunt had agreed. Then Aunt Judith and her brother (Lori's husband) took Evelyn to dinner and then drank alcohol. Evelyn felt disappointed, but uncomfortable about wanting to leave because her father was there. After talking it over with her mom (Lori), they agreed that the next time she went to dinner with her aunt that she would take cab fare so she could leave if her aunt ordered a drink. Evelyn also wrote her father a letter explaining how she had felt and asking him to support her if there was a next time.

Lori was annoyed with her husband because he had known about Aunt Judith's agreement and didn't say anything when they went to dinner and ordered drinks. Lori felt he had betrayed his daughter and told him so. He responded that he was surprised that it was such an issue.

Lori felt that that Evelyn's taking a taxi was merely a stop-gap measure and then reported to me that the difficulty in the family had not been resolved. Because her kids had said they didn't want to be at a party with their aunt, she still felt she needed to talk to Aunt Judith. The opportunity presented itself when they were a planning a joint birthday celebration for the father-in-law. Lori looked at her sister-in-law and said, "My kids aren't going to want to attend if there's a lot of drinking going on." When Judith asked why, Lori said, "Judith, when you drink too much you become sarcastic and tease the kids, and they don't like it. I don't think you realize how much it hurts their feelings. They have told me that they don't want to come to the party if you are drinking." Judith responded defensively and despite her best efforts, Lori knew that she hadn't been able to listen enough to allow Judith to shed her hostility.

In the manner of family dramas, Judith called her brother and complained to him that Lori was blowing things all out of proportion. Fortunately, he had been listening to his kids and listening to Lori assist Evelyn in figuring out what to do next time Aunt Judith invited her to dinner. While he had previously stated that he didn't find Judith's behavior a problem, his perception had changed. His suggestion to Judith was that maybe things would be smoother if she just didn't drink at the party.

And she didn't. They had a great party. Lori has relaxed about the family events. While the behavior of the difficult person hasn't changed completely, Judith said she was willing not to drink when the family gets together. Lori was adamant about not being in Judith's business by resisting the urge to tell Judith to stop drinking completely. Lori just wanted to enjoy the party with her kids.

If Judith ever wants to know more, Lori or her husband might be resources for her in describing what they have seen her do or heard her say. She is still drinking but not when they are at Judith's home, and she has stopped making sarcastic comments to the children.

When an addiction plays a role in someone's difficult behavior, then a different kind of intervention needs to take place. There are many resources for that and the process I am sharing in this book can help someone become clear about what they want to say to an addict. If your difficult person is an addict, I recommend Alcoholics Anonymous or Narcotics Anonymous and their related organizations for family members, Al-Anon and Nar-Anon.

Are My Habits Helping or Hurting?

Other barriers in the way of communicating with our difficult person are our own habits. Dr. Glasser identified habits that can be helpful or hurtful in relationships.

Toxic habits include: Criticizing, Blaming, Complaining, Nagging, Threatening, Punishing, and Bribing. If we are doing any of these things, we are sure to kill a relationship and will feel unhappy. It's also probable that we are actually difficult, ourselves. I certainly experienced some of these habits as I grew up and practiced them too. Criticizing, complaining and blaming were my toxic habits of choice. We have to pay attention to these habits if we are going to be able to converse with our difficult person. Focus on eliminating them.

Dr. Glasser also listed seven caring habits that will build relationships. They are: Supporting, Encouraging, Listening, Accepting, Trusting, Respecting, and Negotiating Differences. I was lucky to have colleagues and friends who practiced these habits, and Denise certainly demonstrated them, too. Keep them in mind as something you want to be practicing, as you are tempted to label your difficult person's behaviors or complain about them.

Remember, we are all attempting to meet our five basic needs, the primary one of which is to feel accepted. When we support, encourage, listen, and acknowledge others, we will start to feel better about the other people in our world. We will feel better because we will meet our own needs for belonging, freedom, achievement and fun. Isn't it fun that by doing something to make relationships better, we actually are doing things that will make us happy? Sneaky, too, isn't it?

Exercise Five

1. Look at your list of impacts and ask yourself, whose business am I in? Am I in my business, the difficult person's business, or God's business?
2. Identify and write down why it is your business to have the conversation with the difficult person.
3. Pay attention to your conversations with others for the next few days. How often do you practice the toxic habits? How often do you practice the caring habits? Do you notice how you feel when you perform one or the other?

CHAPTER EIGHT

SUPPORT YOUR DIFFICULT PERSON

Is This Negative Criticism?

My mentor and friend, Dr. Sidney B. Simon, wrote the magnificent book, *Negative Criticism and What You Can Do about It*. What is often shared as constructive criticism, he designates as "constrictive crudicism," by which he means, useless hurtful information. When a correction becomes a personal attack, it is negative criticism. A hint: absolute comments that include the words, "you always" or, "you never" are usually negative criticism. Often our critical statements come in pairs, and then a third one is introduced by, "...and furthermore..."

We have already seen how we are inclined to judge and criticize another person's behavior. Sid states that when we feel compelled to give someone feedback or a correction, that we need to examine it to see if it is really negative criticism by putting it through the following Six Filters.

First Filter: Is it possible that the person has heard it before? If the answer is yes and the person is still doing it, what's the purpose of saying it again? Marie told me more than once that I intimidated her, but I never understood what she was really saying. I heard negative criticism, and I wasn't open to considering that she actually was intimidated.

Second Filter: Is the other person actually able to change? Has the person tried to change before? My supervisors usually knew I was in some form of therapy and one actually recommended the three visits to a counselor that the agency paid for to help me with my "anger" problem. I didn't believe I had an anger problem so the visits were not very effective. Despite visiting many skillful therapists over the years, I didn't know what behavior to change.

Third filter: Is the other person in any shape to hear it? Is this the best time to actually say something negative to them? About three years before Denise spoke to me, I had become sober in a Twelve-Step program, and I was finally in better shape to hear her statement. I had learned that I didn't have all the answers and didn't need to have them. Her description was so concrete and so obvious that I didn't argue with Denise.

Fourth Filter: How much of my negative feeling is my own "stuff?" Have I asked myself, "Who does the difficult person remind me of?" As I have already pointed out, we need to clarify whether what we feel right now is rooted in the past. Is it possible that the passion of our feeling is inherited from the past experience? We have to figure this out before addressing the present. If we are looking at the present through the hurt of the past, it isn't about the difficult person. It is about us.

Fifth Filter: Am I willing to stick around and pick up the pieces after I deliver my message? Am I willing to be there, in support of the other? It will probably take some time. Nobody likes to receive what feels like criticism no matter how clearly or nonjudgmentally it is stated. If we already are annoyed by our difficult person and want to talk to them, are we willing to listen, converse, and actually dialogue? Think of the mother and daughter conversation you just read. It took some time. Do we value our difficult person or the relationship enough to take the time?

Sixth Filter: Isn't it possible that what this person needs is more validation? Dr. Simon instructs us to use the language of validation that speaks to what we find of value in the other person. This is different from praise. Praise often starts out with, "You are...." and includes a positive judgment about the other person: "You are skilled," or "You are beautiful," or "You are a lovely person." Praise can be disagreed with by the receiver who might think, "No, I'm not."

Validations start with "I" and describe how "I" perceive the other person. The stems are many: "I love...." "I admire..." "I appreciate ..." "I honor..." "I cherish..." or "I respect..." The validations speak to what I see and honor in the other person. It's my opinion, and the other person can tell me I have a wacky opinion, but it is still about me and my perception.

A validation can purely say what we value in the other person: "I love how I laugh with you," or "I respect how you deal with the chaos of children," or "I admire the positive way you tackled that task," or "I enjoy hearing your stories. I learn much from you." The person receiving the validation may be surprised or confused by the information, but they can't argue with it because it is what *you* value in them. They may think, "Well, you are a little strange," but they can't say, "No, I'm not," because you haven't made a statement about them, but about yourself.

Another person's validation has a way of sticking with us, especially if we never thought of ourselves as another does. For example, I heard, "I admire your grace," and thought, "Grace? Me? Graceful? Hah!" Later that day, I remembered and felt graceful when walking. It changed my perception of myself. Validations are powerful statements.

When we really want to criticize, a validation can help us look at the other person differently. Instead of saying, "All you ever do is disagree with me...I am sick of it," a validation might address the same activity but make no judgments. For example, "I respect the way you know what you like and don't like and express it so clearly." Instead of, "Stop trying to control me," you might say, "I appreciate that you care deeply about what I do." Instead of saying, "Stop nitpicking things to death," you could say, "I admire how you clarify all the details."

I have found these Six Filters valuable in helping me change the way I look at another person who I think is doing something wrong. These help me discover when I am in their business.

Exercise Six

1. Check what you have been tempted to say to your difficult person and put it through the Six Filters.
2. Look at your list of what you admire about your difficult person and write out what a validation would look like. Find something to admire about the characteristic that drives you crazy. What can you treasure about this person?

Active Listening

In discussing the possibility of a conversation with the difficult person, workshop participants usually respond, "Yeah, but he'll go ballistic," or "She will get scary angry with me," or "She will cry and play the victim."

Being able to listen means being prepared for an emotional reaction and being willing to allow it, accept it and not criticize it. This is what Dr. Simon calls being willing to stick around and pick up the pieces. This is what Jim did for Tom in the conversation at work.

Dr. Gordon called this process "Active Listening." Here is one of his examples: A young girl comes home and faces her mother, drops her backpack on the floor and cries out, "Nobody likes me. I have no friends. I wish I were anybody but me!" What would you say to her?

Most of us would want to pick her up and say something like, "Oh, my darling; I love you. I like you. I am your friend. You are the most precious, most wonderful girl. You are a gift in my life. How could you wish to be anybody else?"

It is instinctive to want to contradict strong emotions or to talk another person out of them. We have been taught that strong feelings are frightening. Interestingly enough, contradicting another's feelings isn't what really helps. What helps is the ability to listen to the feelings beneath what is actually said. Counselors and social workers learn to "actively listen" as a way of creating safety and acceptance. Dr. Gordon taught his parents how to do this; I have taught parents, volunteer coordinators and workshop participants how to do this.

Our fear of strong emotions leads us to want to comfort someone and tell them it isn't so bad, that things will get better and they don't have to feel pain. But what they hear is, "You shouldn't feel that way," and what that tells them is that we aren't comfortable with their feelings and there's something wrong with them. It creates barriers to communication because we are no longer a need-fulfilling person for them. They don't have the feeling of belonging, which is the strongest genetic need.

If we were to actively listen to the little girl described above, we might say, "Golly, you are upset," or "Wow, you sound really sad," or "Sweetie, I hear that you are really angry and disappointed." Any one of these comments will allow her to know that we actually are tuned in to her emotion, and we aren't scared. She will confirm whether she is scared, angry, or disappointed, so we can acknowledge that with, "Feels pretty strong, huh?" and allow her to explain when she is ready.

Identifying the feeling is the first step. After acknowledging the feeling, it is also possible to listen without saying anything. Making eye contact with the other person and allowing them time to say and feel what they are feeling, without interrupting, is very accepting. Being silent and giving them time to feel can be helpful here too. I have observed my son and daughter-in-law when their two-year-old daughter starts to cry. Whichever adult is closest sits with her and makes eye contact; they don't try to reassure her or change her mind. She stops crying very quickly and moves on to the next interesting activity.

An example of active listening was when I had said something in anger to a client who had hired my agency to do a presentation. I snarled an unfriendly comment to her as I left after the presentation and she reported it to my supervisor, who called me in for a chat. He had every reason to be furious with me. I had been completely inappropriate. I knew it as soon as I had done it and I thought I might be fired.

When he asked me what I had done, I admitted what I had said and explained that I knew there wasn't any excuse. I shared my frustrations with the client. She hadn't done any of the things we had agreed that she would do to prepare the participants for the training and her equipment didn't work. Still, I knew I hadn't acted professionally.

James, my boss, was accepting when he assured me that I wasn't going to get fired, although a note would be placed in my personnel file. He said, "I can tell you are upset and angry." He recognized how it can be frustrating when we show up to do training and find the organization totally unprepared. He asked me what I wished I had done instead and asked me what I could do to refrain from getting so angry the next time it happened. As we talked, he shared some of his horror stories with clients and also shared a time when he had been invited to reconsider something he had done that sparked a client complaint.

I felt safe in the discussion of my behavior, I felt understood and appreciated by James, and I felt that he was in my corner. I realized that his actions made me more committed to having his program be successful. I also knew I wouldn't exhibit that behavior again.

He actively listened to what I was feeling as well as what I said about my behavior and the client. He agreed about how frustrating it can be when clients haven't lived up to their commitments. He heard my anger at the client and restated it to me as disappointment, which was not only accurate, but it also put us together on the same side. It dissolved my rant of all the things the client hadn't done, and it gave me permission to be disappointed, a professional emotion. This created a feeling of safety for me—he understood how I felt because he had felt it too—and it was ok for me to feel it.

James addressed a difficult person by listening to what I was feeling, accepting it, and sharing his experiences with me. I felt okay about the correction and never forgot it.

Often the reaction that concerns us the most is anger. Dr. Gordon has said that anger is the tip of the iceberg and what underlies it is usually fear. We may not have considered the possibility that our difficult person is fearful. Note the times in my story that I feared losing my job.

Nobody likes being told that what they are doing is a problem. Nobody. The first thought is often, "What's wrong with me? I am a bad person," which Dr. Brown defines as a shame tape. Shame is a prevalent feeling in our culture and in her book, *Daring Greatly*, she teaches how to build shame resilience. Empathy: "simply listening, holding space, without judgment, emotionally connecting, and communicating that incredibly healing message of, "You're not alone." (p.81)

As the conversation starter and the listener, we need to use empathy to help the difficult person build that resilience. That is done by listening to the feelings, acknowledging the feelings, and pointing out that it is the behavior that is the problem, not the person. Finally, we empathize with the difficult person as James did with me, acknowledging that he wasn't perfect either.

There may be other fearful thoughts like, "They've all been talking about me," or "Everybody is mad at me." No matter what is said, the response will likely be defensive. Can you listen and respond to the feelings?

A response might be, "You sound scared," or "You're feeling scared. You are not in trouble here." Another response might be: "Sounds like you think I am angry with you. I'm not," or, "So you're really surprised that I am talking about this, eh?" It may require several listening responses before the fear is dissipated. Remember empathy. Remind the difficult person that their behavior is the problem, not them, the person.

Then the next part of the listening statement is: "This isn't personal. Do you know you often do this?" Do they know they do it? Do they know it has a negative impact? Listening and repeating that the behavior is difficult and is having a negative impact will help. Tell the difficult person that there's nothing wrong with them—it is their behavior that is a problem.

If they don't understand or don't agree that they do this behavior, you may need to play the role of coach and ask if you can point it out to them the next time the behavior occurs, as Denise did with me. If you can get an agreement to that, stop there and continue the conversation the next time the difficult person acts the way that you find difficult.

Or, if there is agreement that the behavior occurs, as there was with James, continue the conversation.

"Did you know it has this impact? Is that what you want?"

You can reassure them as much as you can while pointing out the consequences of not changing. Then restate both the emotion you hear as well as the information that you have identified. Dialogue with the difficult person. Listen to the excuses, the tears, and the anger as much as is needed. Remind them that you are there to help them consider changing an impact.

Dialogue.

Listen.

Exercise Seven

1. Think about your difficult person's behaviors. List the emotions you hear from them. Are they angry? Sad? Disappointed? Aloof? Distrustful? Afraid? Make an effort to name an emotion that isn't limited to happy or unhappy. Dig a little deeper.
2. Listen around you and identify when someone is actively listening to another and responding to the content when they are sharing ideas. Are they having a dialogue, rather than arguing? Make a list of when you hear someone listening to another person's feelings. Can you find them in a movie? On a TV show? Do you hear them at work? At play?
3. Who do you hear that seems to be good at it? What does that person say?

In Their Corner

After you have practiced some listening, I invite you to consider how you can be "in their corner." Can you see yourself in the role of the person standing behind the boxer, who sponges his face when the bell rings, puts a drink in his mouth, and cares for his cuts and bruises?

To have a successful conversation with a difficult person, we need to look at the difficult person as someone on our team, not against us, and someone we want to support. We need to see ourselves as someone who is cheering for the difficult person, supporting them to think about what can be changed so their difficult behavior is modified or no longer occurs. We need to be prepared to spend some time with the difficult person, just as we would if we were in the boxer's corner. The difficult person is no longer the enemy. The need for belonging is primary, remember, and being in someone's corner will be perceived by that someone as need-fulfilling.

When we get ready to talk to a difficult person about their behavior, we have to identify the behavior and its impact, and we have to make sure we aren't making the other the enemy or someone from our past. We have to make sure we are in our own business, consider if we can be in their corner, and, finally, explore whether we can actively listen to their feelings. If we decide that we can, indeed, listen to them and stay firm in our understanding of what we are doing, then it's time for the conversation.

Make sure you have given yourselves enough time for a real conversation and that you won't be interrupted during the conversation. Begin by thanking the person for talking to you, express your concern and make the statement of behavior and impact.

You have described the behavior without judgment, you have identified your impression of the other person, you have clarified the impact, you have made sure your "stuff" isn't engaged, and you can actively listen. Will the difficult person instantly say, "Oh, gee whiz, I had no idea. I will stop."? Probably not. You will need to do some active listening and then remind them that you are in their corner.

Be persistent and accepting. Practice the Caring Habits. Don't allow the reaction to sway you.. Stay with your statement of behavior and impact. Keep asking, "Is this what you want?"

Reach for something you can agree on, even if it is only to come talk about this again, with an agreement that neither of you will talk to anybody else about it. This should provide some kind of safety for the difficult person if they think everyone has been talking about them.

Hang in there. Don't give up easily. Remember, tears are reactions to feelings, not facts. Being in someone's corner is more possible if we:

- have spent time letting go of our judgments as we describe the behavior,
- have clarified the impact and consequences of the behavior,
- we have identified our impression of the other person,
- have spelled out how much of our reaction is fact and how much is feeling,
- determined who the difficult person reminds us of and identified that the difficult person is not that person,
- know we are truly "in our own business,"
- are approaching the difficult person using caring habits rather than toxic habits,
- have walked our criticism through Sid's Six Filters,
- have discovered and listed validations for the difficult person,
- have recorded examples of other people using active listening and dialogue to resolve conflict,
- are ready to practice telling them the information and listening to their response, and
- are willing to be in the difficult person's corner to resolve the issue.

Many people were in my corner in my lifetime although I don't think I realized it. Certainly, my mother tried to be, and my aunt and uncle reached out to help me feel accepted and loved. I recall a camp counselor to whom I was so attached that she invited me to her wedding, and my mother and I drove to Connecticut to attend when I was nine. My mother-in-law, who was a warm, smart, loving woman, always welcomed me with open arms. The professors for whom I teach have only given me positive feedback. Friends in workshops and students have given me validations that I have learned to allow in and to believe. Members of the Twelve-Step program who reminded that "Whatever it is, it don't matter," and "Let go and let God." Yet the people who really helped me identify the difficult behavior were Denise, James, and Diane. They were really in my corner at a time when others couldn't be. Each of them was professional, clear, accepting, uncritical, and straightforward in their messages. They didn't dance around the issue, they weren't trying to be in my business, and they wanted me to know what I was doing and how it impacted others. The information changed my life.

Claire's Story

Claire is fifty-five years old, and her friend Jillian is seventy. They serve on the same committee at church, and Claire is the new chair. Jill founded the committee, and is an honorary member. She comes to every meeting and has strong opinions that she frequently shares.

C: Hi, Jill. Thanks for coming to meet me.

J: Well, I'm sure you have questions about being chair and how the committee should be run.

C: I am always happy to hear your ideas and suggestions, Jill. You are a fixture on the committee, and we owe you a tremendous debt of gratitude. I wonder if you are aware that you often ask questions and tell stories about the early days and the meeting gets too long to complete its business. Do you know you do that?

J: Well, I see it as my responsibility to educate everyone on how the organization grew, and so, yes, I tell stories. I am like the historian of the committee.

C: What I wonder about though is: do you realize that doing it at every meeting means we rarely finished an agenda last year? The stories are fascinating but they take time, and I am determined to make the meetings crisp and focused so we can get through the agenda every time.

J: Humph.

C: I wanted to talk to you about this here, not in front of the whole committee. I value you, and I love you, and I want you to know that we need to be able to move on. The impact of your questions and stories is that people leave before votes are taken, and the meetings run too late. Many of our members work a full day before coming to the meeting, and they like to get home to say good night to their families.

J: So, you don't want me to ask any questions.

C: Of course you can ask questions. But think about it, Jill—aren't your questions lead-ins to some story or other?

J: Well, you should know the history of why we do things.

C: I agree, but not at every meeting. We can't get our work done. I don't know if you're aware, but some people stopped attending meetings last year because they ran too long.

J: Of course I noticed, and I thought they should be invited to step down from the committee.

C: The thing is, they want to serve, and they care about the committee and its work, but they don't want to come to meetings that end up lasting two hours when a good portion of that time is listening to stories.

J: SO YOU WANT ME TO QUIT, DO YOU?! WELL, I NEVER—I FOUNDED THIS COMMITTEE!

C: No, Jill, I don't want you to quit. I hear you feeling insulted. That's not what I want at all. I want you to stay. I care about you and value you and so does everybody else. We want your input; we just don't have time for all the stories.

J: But if you don't hear them you might change the committee or something.

C: Yes, well, I don't have any intention of changing the mission of the committee, but it's possible that we might develop some new programs. Would that be so awful?

J: Well, I started most of them so you must think I am old and outdated. I guess I should quit.

C: That's not what we want Jill; honestly it's not what I want. I love you and care about you and expect you to be on this committee for many years to come. I also don't think you stand in the face of change, do you? You've got email and a cell phone—heck you're on Facebook. C'mon, I remember your story about how you helped the church get video screens for the sanctuary. How can you suggest you are outdated?

J: You don't want me to talk in meetings, and now you want to change the committee.

C: I want you to speak to the issue on the table, not tell us how it was handled in the past. The committee is changing the format so that the members can attend for just an hour. This is the nature of the volunteers in our church today. They want to conduct business.

J: This is progress?

C: You know what? I am sensing you fear we will throw the baby out with the bathwater. You know so many stories about our church—shouldn't we write them down? What if we had a night where you told your stories and we recorded them, and someone transcribed them, and then we had a history?

J: Instead of a committee meeting?

C: No, no—this is bigger. I'm thinking it would be for the whole church. And some of your compatriots could talk too, about their memories. I'll bet a lot of folks would come to hear these stories. We all want to know what the church was like twenty, forty, fifty years ago.

J: Well, that sounds like fun, actually. I'm sure I can get some folks to tell some stories, besides mine.

C: Jill, let's you and me talk to the education minister tomorrow, ok? I think we have a really good idea. Please don't quit the committee.

J: Ah, you can't get rid of me that easily, haha.

In this dialogue, Claire was in Jill's corner. She was personally connected to Jill, but knew her committee members were going to quit if she didn't get Jill to modify her behavior in the meetings. I think we all quake in our boots when we have to say to someone that because of progress, their ways of doing things need to change too. We fear resistance and we avoid telling people about the impact of their behavior.

Notice that Claire listened to Jill's reactions. She accepted them and reminded Jill that "the times they are a-changing," and she is changing with them. Claire resisted getting angry when Jill did, acknowledged her fear, and remained positive. She was in Jill's corner as she repeated her main points about meeting duration, and her desire for Jill to stay on the committee. Claire didn't get "hooked," and they arrived at a mutually amicable solution.

When Jill got angry, Claire responded to her fear with, "I hear you feeling insulted." She went on to say that she didn't want Jill to quit, that she cared about Jill and wanted her to stay. It may be that you won't be in a position to say, "I love you and care about you," but you will want to address what you like about your difficult person so they don't think you are just out to get them. It is important to separate the behavior from the person.

In situations like this one, where someone's behavior is disrupting an entire committee or work team or family, remember that no matter what you think you see and hear, inside, the difficult person feels a sense of disconnectedness and often has no understanding of what they say or do that pushes people away. Many of us are unaware of what we say and do. We aren't aware of our impact and how others perceive us. The difficult person's obliviousness is just more obvious.

CHAPTER NINE

DOES IT WORK?

*You cannot force someone to comprehend a message
that they are not ready to receive. Still, you must
never underestimate the power of planting a seed.*
- Animus Novo

D ifficult people are usually willing to change when they learn about the problem and the consequences of not changing. I have had some counseling professionals say to me, "Some people don't want to

119

change. They like being difficult." My reaction is that this is because a real consequence that impacts the difficult individual has not been identified. It is more important to fulfill whatever need they are fulfilling than to avoid whatever consequence is imminent. So yes, it can happen.

Julie's Story

My friend Julie talked to me over coffee about some problems she was having with her new boss. Julie loved learning all the ins-and-outs of the computerized system at her new job. She understood that it would take a while to learn, but found it really frustrating that her boss didn't spend the time to teach her new skills. Her boss often sat down, showed the steps, and then walked away. Not only that, she would make comments in front of other staff like, "Ah well, the newbie. Let me show you again," in a patronizing tone.

As we talked about the situation, Julie identified that her boss would sit and do the work for her instead of coaching her through the commands, so Julie was watching her do things, not getting to do them herself. She felt it was taking much longer to learn because her boss said things like, "I don't have time to watch, let me just show you."

Julie acknowledged that she was flattered that her boss thought she could learn that quickly but it wasn't happening. She also was depressed because her boss appeared to use negative criticism as a motivator and Julie didn't want to work in that kind of an environment. It was too soon to look for another job, and her work schedule was perfect for the other parts of Julie's life. She was beginning to dread going to work and really wanted to know what to do.

I pointed out that it was probable that her boss had no idea of what she was doing. I suggested maybe having a conversation about it. What was the worst that could happen? If the boss continued to make fun of her, it hadn't worked. If she listened, maybe they could agree on some kind of resolution.

Julie is a thoughtful person who has done a good deal of personal-growth work, including Byron Katie's "The Work," and she understood what I was saying, so she was interested. We role-played the conversation with me being her (Julie) and Julie being the boss. I said things like, "When you show me the solution, it takes me longer to learn, and I end up not being able to serve our customers in a professional manner." That described the behavior and an impact to which her boss could relate.

I also said, "I feel hurt when you use sarcasm and make fun of me, calling me the newbie, and that also hinders my ability to learn quickly and serve the clients effectively."

As her boss, Julie said things like, "Oh, you're too sensitive," and "I can't take the time to watch you do the steps; I'm too busy," and "Don't you want to work here?" I responded with statements like, "So, you're afraid it was a mistake to hire me?" and, "Yes, I want to work here; this job is fascinating." Then I asked, "Is there someone else who can teach me the steps so I don't have to bother you?" and then I pointed out, "You told me when you hired me that you wanted my sensitive energy in your workspace. Have you changed your mind?"

Because we had role-played, and because Julie was comfortable being in her boss' corner, the actual conversation was successful, with the boss thanking her for the feedback. She ended up taking more time with Julie and the sarcasm disappeared. It was interesting that after about a year, the boss again started exhibiting the same sarcasm and negative behavior to all the staff. Julie initiated the conversation again, and again her boss lessened the criticism. When it began again about six months later, Julie felt comfortable finding another job. Her boss didn't value her work and Julie enough to maintain the behavior change; some difficult people never change.

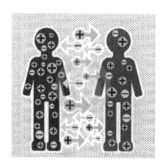

Energy Anyone?

On the other hand, many workshop participants report that, by doing the strategies in the workshop, they started to look at the difficult person in a different way and the problem wasn't as great as it seemed before. Some situations seemed to resolve even before the conversation, simply due to the change in perspective caused by preparing for the conversation.

I think it has something to do with the energy between people, which we can't see but know it is there. When we start looking at the difficult person differently, our attitudes change and they seem to be different.

If that's too "woo-woo" for you, consider that by working through these questions and preparing for the conversation, your perception of the difficult person will change. This new perception may influence your micro-behaviors and non-verbal cues, which your difficult person may pick up consciously or subconsciously.

In the next chapter, you are encouraged to practice with a partner who will role-play the difficult person. If you listen to the feelings, you become a need-fulfilling person for them. The need for belonging is primary, remember. Describe the behavior and its impact and ask if they are aware they are doing the behavior. You aren't criticizing, you are asking, and you are listening to their reactions.

The energy will shift. Guaranteed.

CHAPTER TEN

PREPARATION

Rehearse

At this point, if you have been doing the suggested writing work of the book, you have prepared the elements for the conversation with your difficult person. You have identified the specific behavior and the impact that causes problems, you have isolated the reasons you value the difficult person, and you have written a validation for that person. You have determined that you are in your own business and not just wanting to change the other person because of a personal issue of your own. You have paid attention to how to listen to their feelings and hopefully practiced it with others in your life. It is time to consider having the conversation.

Give yourself at least three weeks to prepare:

1. The first week, take the time to consider the difficult person every morning. Ask yourself, "How do these problems come up? Is it the same every time? When has it been different?" Write down anything you want to remember. Ask yourself if there is something in the environment or the system that could be changed to help alleviate the issue.

2. The second week, number from one to twenty on the left side of a piece of paper and list the rebuttals you think the difficult person might have to your statement. Record the excuses they might give or all the ways they will blame other people. Draw a vertical line down the middle of the page, and start to list all the responses you might give to these comments if you are in their corner. What emotions might you acknowledge, and what can you say that allows the difficult person the right to their feelings? Keep going. List them all. Then use this list in the next step.

3. The third week, practice. This is a time when practice makes life easier. Have you ever done a practice interview with a friend before a job interview? It is the opportunity to respond to the hard questions you have thought of, and some you

haven't thought of. It gives you a chance to think quickly and make mistakes. You can back up and start over. Ask a friend to help you practice this conversation. Give your list to your friend so you get a variety of responses, and keep a copy for yourself in case you get stuck. Invite your practice partner to go through all the listed responses. Then have them respond in as many new ways as possible that are not listed. This is an opportunity to react to a statement or question you might not be expecting. Say your statement and have your friend respond in the way that you fear—roaring defensiveness. Practice listening to the defensive statements and the fear of your difficult person.

Remember you are aiming for a conversation, not a confrontation. You are not setting out to slap the other person with your opinion. It's not an argument. It is not negative criticism. It is not manipulation. It is a conversation. You want the difficult person to succeed. They are no longer the enemy. The art of dialogue and negotiation may appear to be lost in our culture today, but this is what you will want to think about as you prepare.

Pointers

As you have worked through the weekly steps and practiced, and are getting ready to have a conversation, keep these pointers in mind:

Don't Expect Immediate Compliance. If you can even achieve a grudging acceptance to have you point out their behavior the next time they do it, you have achieved a great deal.

Take a Pause. During the conversation give yourself a chance to stop reacting to the other person. Think of a red button, similar to the Staples EASY button. See this as a PAUSE button and mentally push it during the conversation.

Give Yourself a Chance to be Curious. Ask yourself: Where is the good here? What can I learn here? How can I be in their corner here?

Don't Get Hooked. Be accepting of their reactions and possible tears—tears are healing. Remember you are there to help them succeed, so listen to the feelings under the tears if you can, or sit in accepting silence until they can talk again. Remind your difficult person what you value about them and why you are having the conversation.

When in Doubt, Summarize. If you can restate what you said and how the other reacted, it can give you both a chance to reflect. You can see where the conversation is going and remind the difficult person that it isn't a personal attack. It also tends to help you ask, again, "Is this what you really want?"

Guide for Statements in Conversation

1 I AM CONCERNED ABOUT (our customers/my admin/my kids/our work team/ the volunteers) _____

2 DID YOU KNOW THAT YOU...
   - referred to my admin as "your girl"
   - argued with a customer about a price
   - yelled at our boss to keep his voice down outside your cubicle so you could hear your caller
   - called my son an egghead and teased him about getting good grades
   - tell us in our meetings what "you" need to do, not making it a "we" proposition
   - raise your voice when someone disagrees with you
   - are consistently late with your projects
   - _____

3 DO YOU KNOW THAT YOU DO THIS?
   - I hear that you think it is someone else's fault, but it is your behavior that I am talking about. Do you know that you do this?

- It sounds like you think I am picking on you. Honestly? I AM IN YOUR CORNER on this and wasn't sure if you knew you do this.
- (If they don't acknowledge the behavior) Do you want me to point it out next time?

4 ARE YOU AWARE OF THE IMPACT OF THIS BEHAVIOR ON...(my admin, the customer and sales, your job security, my son, our volunteer team, me getting my job done) _____

5 IS THIS THE IMPACT THAT YOU WANT? (I don't think you are doing this on purpose, are you?)
- SO YOU THINK THE OTHER PERSON SHOULD REACT DIFFERENTLY?
- DO YOU THINK YOU CAN CHANGE ANOTHER PERSON?

6 DO YOU KNOW THAT THE CONSEQUENCE OF YOUR BEHAVIOR is that ....
- customers leave,
- admins file grievances,
- my boss thinks I run a poor department,
- my son refuses to come to your party,
- the volunteers want me to fire you
- I am late completing my projects
- _____

7 Sounds like you think the impact is the other person's problem but actually, it isn't. It is mine and yours. We can't change another person, we can only change ourselves. I WOULD LIKE TO HAVE A DIFFERENT IMPACT, AND FOR THAT, WE NEED A DIFFERENT BEHAVIOR.

8 HOW DO YOU FEEL?
- you think I am picking on you

- you were having a bad day
- you think I have always disliked you
- you think the other person deserved to be spoken to that way
- you feel attacked
- you feel misunderstood
- _____

8   I HEAR YOU AND UNDERSTAND THAT YOU FEEL THIS WAY. NEVERTHELESS, YOUR BEHAVIOR CREATES THIS IMPACT, AND THIS IS THE CONSEQUENCE:

_____

9   IS THIS WHAT YOU WANT?
10 CAN WE TALK ABOUT IT?

EPILOGUE

What about Me?

All people have a need to belong, to have fun, to have a sense of making choices, to be healthy, and to have a sense of empowerment and achievement. If changing the behavior doesn't increase one's ability to meet needs, well, maybe they won't change. I didn't want to get fired, and I wanted to keep earning money to meet my need for survival. Also, I loved the teaching I did in my job; it met my need for fun and freedom. I was able to continue meeting these needs by ending the tantrums at work and, finally, in many other areas of my life.

The process of change is a series of little steps. I am much more aware of when I am acting difficult, and much more tuned in to other people's reactions, so that, even though I sometimes disappoint myself, these times are fewer.

Recently I was in the midst of preparing for a pot-luck at church. It was early in the morning, and I was hurrying to get the supplies out on the kitchen tables for the volunteers who would hopefully show up soon and help. I was moving quickly, but I wasn't aware of being stressed.

My cell phone rang, and a friend was calling to verify that we were having the meal and asking me if she should bring food. In my head, I thought, "Duh. A pot-luck. Everybody brings food. Why are you calling? How long have you come to pot-lucks here?" My tone probably reflected these thoughts, although I didn't actually say those words. I think I said, "Well, of course. Food is always welcome; bring whatever you want. If you didn't plan ahead, don't worry. There is always enough."

As I ended the call, I realized I hadn't been very friendly. "Damn it," I thought. "I am more stressed than I realized. What am I afraid of? Probably that if the volunteers don't show up, I will have to do this all myself? Okay, but I didn't have to be rude. Ah well, more to work on. Nice to know I'm not perfect yet."

The caller is a close friend who has attended my workshop and knows my story. When she walked through the door thirty minutes later, we hugged, and I apologized for being less than gracious. She said that she had understood, told me we were fine and then proceeded to help set up for the event.

The miracle here is that I recognized that I had been short with her, possibly difficult. Certainly, in my thoughts, I had been rude. I not only recognized it, but I also apologized for it. I am learning to check out my impact on others when I think I have allowed my "difficult" characteristic to respond.

So will your difficult person instantly change? I don't think I changed instantly, but I am gradually more aware of the characteristics of being difficult. I have started noticing other people in my life who appear to be demanding and maybe even bossy. My attitude toward them has entirely changed. They may or may not be difficult people, but I see the similarities between their behavior and mine and I immediately put myself in their corner. If I worry about their motivation or how I want them to be, I remember that I am getting into their business instead of staying in my own business.

When I put myself in their corner, I am much more patient and accepting. The result is that hopefully they feel recognized so their need to demand certain things relaxes and the relationship is eased. I don't give up my boundaries, I am firm about what I will or won't do, but I am aware of how it feels to be demanding and to need things done a certain way. I work to eliminate the friction with them. It is not perfect; I admit there are some people I avoid because I find myself in their business, but I am getting better at staying out of it.

My buttons do get pushed, though. A member of our church choir is chronically behind in understanding where we are in the music. The director will talk about a certain section of the music and how we are going to handle it and just as he starts to lead us through it, this individual will raise a hand and ask, "How are we going to deal with this section?" The director is endlessly patient and loving and re-explains everything. I want to chew nails and bop the choir member over the head, screaming, "Pay attention!" It has become a constant itch to me, and I have to talk to myself to not react. I am not sure who this person reminds me of or why I can't stay out of his business, but there you are—it annoys me.

A week ago, as we were rehearsing, he asked a question that the director had just answered and, without realizing what I was doing, I *answered*. The individual said, "I didn't ask you, Sam. I asked the director," and I realized I was so comfortable from all the singing that I had forgotten to watch out for my "know-it-all" tendency. A year ago, I would have felt deep remorse and sadness that I was so clearly difficult and I would have felt sad that I hadn't changed. This time, I saw that I may want to do some more self-examination around him.

I started the process by laughing to myself. "Oh, whoops. Tee-hee. There I go again. Not perfect yet. More fun to work on." I have found that the best way to react when I find myself being difficult, is to first apologize when necessary, and, secondly, to laugh at myself and say, "Oh goodie, more to do." It is a complete contradiction to my former belief that I don't belong, or that I am inherently flawed and nobody will ever like me.

Laughing at myself is a way to remind myself that nobody is perfect and my journey is ongoing. I can experience something different every time I choose to. It is up to me to choose the thought. When I was growing up, I couldn't laugh at myself because I thought my sisters, and sometimes my mother, were laughing at me and it felt as if they were trying to hurt me. I couldn't laugh at myself because that meant they were winning. Now I know that my life is not a war zone and I can laugh with and at myself. I am free to change as much as I can and as much as I want.

My name is an example of this life process. I had been Sarah for eighteen years and couldn't wait to shed it because, in my mind, Sarah was not welcome. I chose the name Sam when I went to college and told everyone that my name was Samuelle, like Annabelle. I felt totally free to be whoever I wanted to be in college and continued to call myself Sam until it was suggested to me at age thirty-three that I might want to heal the pain of being Sarah. Some close friends at the time pointed out that Sarah includes the cheer, "Rah!" and they began to emphasize that part of my name. I was attending a workshop and each time they saw me at a meal or walking to a session, they would exclaim my name with excitement and joy. They would say, "So good to see you, S*arah*," and, "S*arah*, we're so glad you're here." It was the opposite of my childhood programming and even though it was only for a few days, it helped.

Returning home, I invited all my friends to call me Sarah, although I will always be Aunt Sam to a select few, and I worked at liking myself with that name. Denise corrected Sarah, and Sarah started the process of discovering I was difficult. Finally, at age fifty-five, I chose to return to Sam without hating Sarah. Now I introduce myself as Sam, but I am happy to have people call me Sarah. It means "princess" in Hebrew, and it is a reminder that I am a princess and that I have friends who like me. Sam is someone who enjoys laughing at herself. I love being Gramma Sam, and it is easier to pronounce for those learning English.

I can't promise that your difficult person will learn to laugh at themselves, but you can laugh at yourself and it may ease some tension in the relationship. I *can* promise you that if you ask yourself the questions I have delineated here and answer them honestly enough to have a real conversation with your difficult person, the relationship will change for the better.

I urge you to have the conversation with your difficult person. If you need help, I am an email away at www.sarahelliston.com. I am passionate about helping the difficult people of the world understand what they do to push people away so they can, if they want, make changes. I believe it will lead to happier relationships. I know it will bring more peace into our lives. It has in mine.

Are You Difficult?

After reading this book, it is possible that you are wondering if you might be a difficult person. Perhaps everybody is difficult to someone. Maybe this has been a wake-up call for you. You might be a difficult person if:

- when another person talks to you about your work or your behavior, your first thought is "I don't measure up"
- you often feel other people are dismissing you because of your gender or training or lack of credentials
- you often argue with others
- you feel isolated in your opinions
- you feel that life is a struggle
- you confront others as a natural reaction
- you are angry at least half of the time
- you feel justified in your anger
- you feel that there is never enough
- you complain a good deal of the time

- many of your relationships are estranged
- you often feel defensive

These behaviors may indicate low self-esteem or perfectionism and don't necessarily mean you are a difficult person. If you find yourself answering yes to four or more, you might find it helpful to do further self-examination. My next book will cover this in depth.

People don't resist change. They resist being changed.
- Peter Senge

BIBLIOGRAPHY

Brown, Brené. *Daring Greatly: How the Courage to Be Vulnerable Transforms the Way We Live, Love, Parent, and Lead.* New York: Penguin, 2012.

Glasser, William. *Choice Theory; A New Psychology of Personal Freedom.* New York: Harper Perennial, 2011.

Glasser, William. Glasser, Carleen. *Getting Together and Staying Together.* New York: Harper Collins, 2000.

Gordon, Thomas. *Parent Effectiveness Training: The Proven Program for Raising Responsible Children.* New York: Random House, 2000.

Katie, Byron and Stephen Mitchell. *Loving What Is: Four Questions That Can Change Your Life.* New York: Penguin, 2003.

Senge, Peter. *The Fifth Discipline: The Art and Practice of the Learning Organization.* Random House, 2006.

Simon, Sidney B., Leland W. Howe, and Howard Kirschenbaum. *Values Clarification.* New York: Warner, 1995.

Simon, Sidney, B. *Negative Criticism and What You Can Do about It.* Argus Communications, 1978.

For Further Study

- Parent Effectiveness Training, Gordon Training International, www.gordontraining.com
- Dr. William Glasser, www.wglasser.com
- Dr. Sidney B. Simon, find his books on www.Amazon.com
- Dr. Brené Brown, Daring Greatly, AVERY, An imprint of Penguin Random House, 2012 www.brenebrown.com
- Byron Katie, www.thework.com
- For help in identifying feelings versus facts, consider www.fastereft.com
- Sarah (Sam) Elliston, www.sarahelliston.com

Sarah (Sam) Elliston
Biography

Sarah (Sam) Elliston is an expert in the art of Dealing with Difficult People. She is a top workshop leader and a member of the faculty of the William Glasser Institute, which espouses "Reality Therapy" to foster behavioral change.

But her instructional career began long before she even became aware that she was herself a "difficult person," traits that began in Lincoln, Massachusetts, where she grew up. For more than 30 years she has been teaching and training, first as a high school teacher in Ohio and Cincinnati—and then as an administrator in the not-for-profit sector.

Elliston, who holds a BA in International Relations from the University of Maine and a Master of Arts in Teaching from Brown University, spent 23 years with United Way's Volunteer Center, coordinating volunteers for city government, training local volunteer coordinators and board volunteers, and managing the volunteer program for United Way.

While at United Way, she developed and managed a certificate-earning series on volunteer management with Northern Kentucky University and the Union Institute. She also taught both undergraduate and graduate courses in Volunteer Program Management at Northern Kentucky University.

Her career at United Way included initiating and managing the Municipal Volunteer Program – Volunteer Cincinnati - for 15 years. In addition, she worked closely with nonprofit agencies to empower their volunteer programs and boards of trustees and served on the Executive Committee of the Cincinnati Association of Volunteer Administrators. She has presented at the International Conference on Volunteer Administration, the Conference for National and Community Service and regional and state conferences in Ohio, Kentucky, Iowa, New York, Michigan and Illinois. She is a Certified Volunteer Administrator, the highest level of professional certification in the field.

In addition to her work as a volunteer administrator, Elliston pursued a course of study that would bring her to her current area of expertise. She is now certified in Values Realization, Parent Effectiveness Training and Reality Therapy. She has served as a board member and president of the Values Realization Institute.

Elliston's passion is training and designing an experience that allows learners to find a process that works for them to make the changes they desire. She is a gentle, persistent, humorous and intelligent trainer, drawing from many sources and always willing to admit that she might not know the answer.

For more info, visit: www.sarahelliston.com